NORTH DOWNS
WAY

NORTH DOWNS WAY

Neil Curtis and Jim Walker

Photographs by Mike Williams

AURUM PRESS
COUNTRYSIDE COMMISSION
Ordnance Survey

Neil Curtis has a degree in geology and has worked in natural history publishing since 1971. He lives in Oxfordshire and runs his own publishing service. He is the author of National Trail Guide no. 4, *The Ridgeway*.
Jim Walker has been the manager of the North Downs Way National Trail since 1996.
Jim Walker's thanks go to everyone who has worked to establish the North Downs Way as a quality trail, much loved by all who use it. Particular thanks go to members of the Management Group, the rights of way officers, other National Trail officers and to Helena, Jacob and Ben Walker.

This edition first published 1992 by Aurum Press Ltd in association
with the Countryside Commission and the Ordnance Survey
This revised edition first published 1998
Text copyright © 1992, 1998 by Aurum Press Ltd, the Countryside
Commission and the Ordnance Survey
Maps Crown copyright © 1992, 1998 by the Ordnance Survey
Photographs copyright © 1992 by the Countryside Commission
Ordnance Survey, Pathfinder and Travelmaster are registered trademarks and
the OS symbol and Explorer are trademarks of Ordnance Survey, the National
Mapping Agency of Great Britain.

A catalogue record for this book is available from the British Library.

ISBN 1 85410 537 X

Book design by Robert Updegraff
Cover photograph: A view across White Downs from Ranmore Common, near
Dorking
Title page photograph: The Wye Downs and
Wye Valley from Soakham Downs

Typeset by Wyvern 21 Ltd, Bristol
Printed and bound in Italy by Printer Srl Trento

CONTENTS

circular walks appear on pages 48, 51, 104 and 144

How to use this guide

This guide to the 156-mile (251-kilometre) North Downs Way is in three parts:

 • The introduction, with an historical background to the area and advice for walkers, horseriders and cyclists.

 • The Trail itself, split into twelve chapters, with maps opposite the description for each route section. The distances noted with each chapter represent the total length of the North Downs Way, including sections through towns and villages. This part of the guide also includes information on places of interest as well as a number of short walks which can be taken around parts of the path. Key sites are numbered both in the text and on the maps to make it easier to follow the route description.

 • The last part includes guidance on sources of information on subjects such as local transport, accommodation and organisations involved with the North Downs Way.

The maps have been prepared by the Ordnance Survey® for this trail guide using 1:25 000 Pathfinder® or Explorer™ maps as a base. The line of the North Downs Way is shown in yellow, with the status of each section of the trail – footpath or bridleway, for example – shown in green underneath (see key on inside front cover). These rights of way markings also indicate the precise alignment of the North Downs Way, which you should follow. In some cases, the yellow line on these maps may show a route that is different from that shown on older maps; you are recommended to follow the yellow route in this guide, which will be the route that is waymarked with the distinctive acorn symbol ♣ used for all National Trails. Any parts of the North Downs Way that may be difficult to follow on the ground are clearly highlighted in the route description, and important points to watch for are marked with letters in each chapter, both in the text and on the maps.

Should there be a need to divert the North Downs Way from the route shown in this guide, for maintenance work or because the route has had to be changed, you are advised to follow any waymarks or signs along the path.

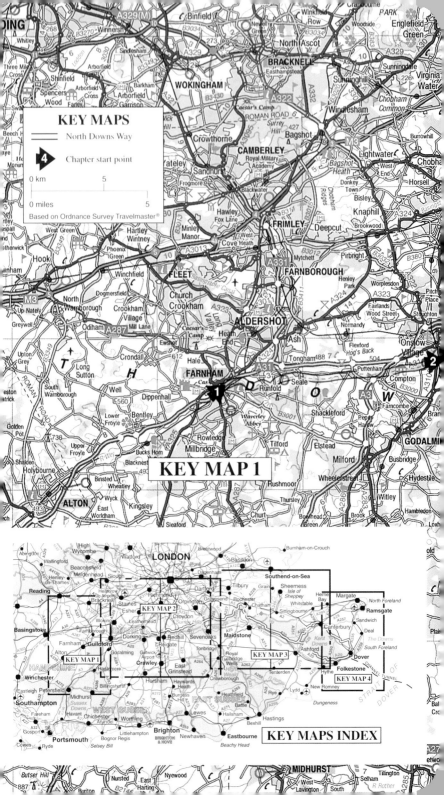

KEY MAPS

North Downs Way

4 Chapter start point

0 km 5

0 miles 5

Based on Ordnance Survey Travelmaster®

KEY MAP 1

KEY MAPS INDEX

KEY MAP 1

KEY MAP 2

KEY MAP 3

KEY MAP 4

KEY MAP 2

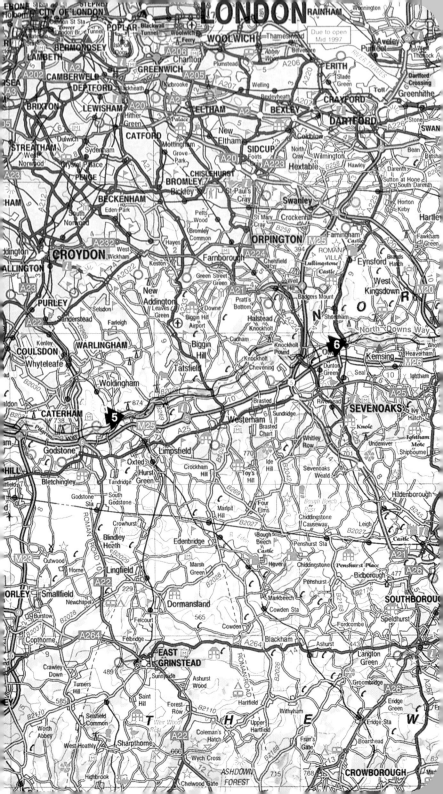

KEY MAP 3

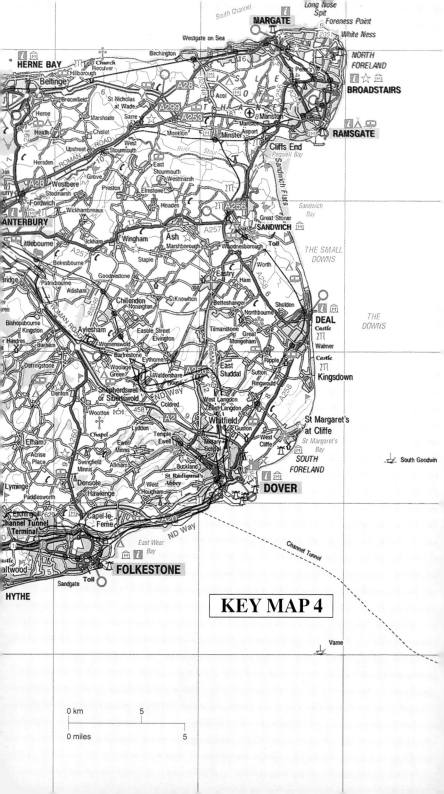

KEY MAP 4

Distance checklist

This list will assist you in calculating the distances between places on the North Downs Way where you may be planning to stay overnight, or in checking your progress along the way.

location	approx. distance from previous location	
	miles	*km*
Farnham	0	0
Puttenham	6.6	10.6
Guildford	4.4	7.1
Newlands Corner	3.4	5.5
Ranmore Common	7.3	11.7
Box Hill (A24)	2.2	3.5
Reigate Hill	7.9	12.7
Merstham	2.2	3.5
Oxted	8.0	12.9
Knockholt Pound	8.3	13.4
Otford	3.4	5.5
Wrotham	6.7	10.8
Medway Bridge	10.6	17.1
Detling	10.0	16.1
Hollingbourne	5.3	8.5
Harrietsham	2.3	3.7
Lenham	1.6	2.6
Charing	4.2	6.6
Boughton Lees	4.7	7.6
Wye	2.3	3.7
Stowting	6.7	10.8
Etchinghill	4.6	7.4
Folkestone (A260)	4.6	7.4
Dover	7.5	12.1
Boughton Lees	0	0
Chilham	5.9	9.5
Chartham Hatch	3.6	5.8
Canterbury (Cathedral)	3.6	5.8
Patrixbourne	3.2	5.1
Shepherdswell	7.2	11.6
Dover	8.5	13.7

Preface

This guidebook directs the user along the North Downs Way National Trail which stretches across south-east England from Surrey to Kent, finishing on the Kent coast at Dover.

National Trails are ideal for long-distance walkers, and the North Downs Way is also suitable for use by cyclists and horseriders on sections of bridleway. In addition, this book suggests some circular walks for day trippers and locals.

The terrain is relatively easy going making it a suitable trail for the whole family to enjoy and there is plenty of opportunity to find food or accommodation en route.

Waymarking and maintenance are carried out by local authorities on behalf of the Countryside Commission and the distinctive acorn symbol signals that you are on the right route.

I hope you will enjoy using this book during many hours of delightful walking on the North Downs Way.

Richard Simmonds
Chairman
Countryside Commission

PART ONE

INTRODUCTION

Pleasures of the North Downs Way

The North Downs Way offers tranquility, rural beauty, historical and literary interest, and some splendid natural history, to anyone willing to make the journey from the Hog's Back to the Kent coast.

Unlike the most popular National Trails, where over-use has led to serious problems of erosion in places along the route, and where you can play 'follow my leader' along some sections, it is perfectly possible, even in the height of the summer holiday season, to spend hours or even days negotiating the North Downs Way without meeting another traveller, except perhaps an occasional dog-walker or local horse and rider. And this is particularly surprising when you recall that the route traverses England's thronging south-eastern quarter, which is networked with trunk roads, motorways and railway lines, and peppered with industry, suburbia and dormitory towns; this does, however, mean that the walker is seldom far from shelter or public transport.

The North Downs Way is 156 miles (251 km) long, but walkers rarely undertake all of this, because there are two options from which to choose at the eastern end. If you walk from close to Farnham's railway station to the docks at Dover using the southern route, you will cover 125 miles (201 km) through Surrey and Kent. The alternative forks north near Boughton Lees, and if you follow this option through Canterbury your route is 131 miles (211 km) long.

Another nice option might be to start at, say, Dover or Canterbury and treat the Kent loop as a circular walk of some 57 miles (91 km).

This book describes the walk from west to east through Surrey and Kent respectively. This means you can begin, conveniently, at Farnham railway station and your journey takes you to the sea – always a satisfying goal and a fitting climax to any walk on the wild side in an island country – and generally, because prevailing winds in Britain blow from the west, you should have any breeze at your back for much of the way to give you that little extra spur.

The North Downs Way is a National Trail of contrasts. For those who, especially on a hot day, prefer to walk or ride beneath the shade of trees, Surrey offers large expanses of beech, oak, ash, juniper and yew woodland. But for others, there are few greater joys than striding across the springy, rabbit-cropped turf on a chalk ridge crest with a light breeze blowing, fine open vistas spread out below, and with the sea a distant blue-grey ribbon between sky and earth. From the Wye Downs across Cheriton Hill and Hangar Down to Creteway Down, the Kentish stretch offers just such inspirational journeying.

You will follow river valleys, such as that of the River Wey, cross others, like that of the River Mole (on stepping stones when the water is not too high), and you will need to haul yourself to heights of more than 655 feet (200 metres) to such nationally famous beauty spots as St Martha's Hill, Box Hill and Newlands Corner. You will walk beside motorways, pass beneath and over them, and you will be taken airily and noisily

The Temple, Reigate Hill, was presented to the Corporation of the Borough of Reigate by Lieutenant-Colonel Robert William Inglis in 1909.

In this view to the west from Reigate Hill, the scarp slope of the North Downs is very evident as it forms a back-stop to the Weald.

across the Medway by the same construction that carries the M2 with haste towards Canterbury. There are homely churches and awe-inspiring cathedrals to admire and to explore. For the literary or artistically minded, there are connections with William Cobbett and George Meredith, with Dickens and Tennyson, and with Graham Sutherland. There are reminders of almost every age of English life – from the prehistoric long barrow of Kit's Coty to the south of Chatham, the possible site of an Iron Age fort at Arthur's Seat near Gravelly Hill, through Roman roads and Norman castles, to medieval churches, sixteenth century mansions, country houses of the 1700s, and right through to the present day.

At the Loseley Park Estate near Guildford, home of the More-Molyneux family since 1562, there are farms that have revived organic dairy and cereal agriculture so successfully that their preservative-free products have now become nationally sought-after. And what could be more traditional than the round tower with its conical chimney of an oast house, formerly used as a kiln for drying the hops that were, and still are, grown all around in the 'garden of England'? There are disused chalk quarries and working lime pits. The Marley Tile works still looks busy enough and as you follow the crest of the ancient cliffs above Folkestone you will look down upon the complex of railway lines and loading ramps that surrounds the entrance to the Channel Tunnel.

Throughout its length, the North Downs Way is a versatile route. It is possible to complete the whole route in a week, or even less, averaging more than 20 miles (32 km) a day. However, unless walking the path is an exercise in stamina, to complete it at a more leisurely and enjoyable pace should take about 10 or 12 days, so that a day's walk is about 12–15 miles (20–25 km). A reasonable pace to maintain is about $2\frac{1}{2}$ miles (4 km) an hour, so 15 miles (25 km) might take a little over six hours. During three seasons of the year, this leaves you plenty of time to stand and stare, to stop for feeding and watering, to chat with companion or with passerby, and to undertake a bit of botany or to explore a cathedral. Even in winter, a day's walk of this distance should be quite feasible. Remember, though, that if you are travelling with a companion or in a party, do not try to attempt more than can reasonably be achieved by the least fit among you. And bear in mind, too, that a steep ascent or crossing a large, freshly ploughed field can slow you considerably.

Nor are you confined to Shanks' pony; there are other ways of travelling lengthy stretches of the North Downs Way. Bridleways (waymarked with blue arrows) can be used by horseriders and cyclists as well as by walkers; and on byways (marked with red arrows) or 'roads used as public paths' (RUPPs), such as the metalled lengths of the Pilgrims' Way, motor vehicles are usually permitted as well. There are circular routes, both official and unofficial, based on parts of its length and up to 8 miles or so (12 km) in distance. It would be possible to take two cars and park one at each end of a day's stretch. Or you might wish to complete the Surrey section and the Kent one as two separate walks.

Remember that, throughout its length, the North Downs Way crosses land that is owned by someone, whether private landlord or farmer, the National Trust, or a trust for nature conservation. The Countryside Commission has spent many years negotiating new rights of way with landowners, and the county councils expend a good deal of time and money in maintaining waymarks and trying to ensure that the rights of way remain open. Their work is not helped by travellers who do not respect the rights and wishes of the people and organisations who have given their consent for paths to cross their land, sometimes at direct personal cost in terms of repairing stiles or limiting their own use of land. So follow the Country Code (see inside back cover).

However you tackle the North Downs Way, it is there to be enjoyed and there is much to enjoy. From ridge top to valley, from shady woodland grove to open chalk downland, from Georgian town to ancient port, a traveller on the North Downs Way will usually have the songs of birds for company but, where hill or screen of trees silences the roads and railways, the silence may be so deep and the solitude so complete that one's own inner musings may sound loud in the mind's ear.

History of the North Downs Way

The North Downs Way National Trail was officially opened at a ceremony in Wye in Kent – appropriately enough by the then Archbishop of Canterbury, The Most Reverend and Right Honourable Donald Coggan – in September 1978, following 15 years of planning and negotiation. The intention of the Countryside Commission, which proposed the route, was for a long-distance way to follow, as nearly as possible, the chalk ridge that forms the North Downs between Farnham and Dover. In this way, travellers on foot and, in some parts, on horse or bicycle could enjoy the delights of the Surrey Hills and Kent Downs, designated as Areas of Outstanding Natural Beauty, in a part of the country that is densely populated.

For eastward travellers, the Way divides at Boughton Lees, near Wye in Kent, and the northern loop proceeds via Canterbury to its destination. Along this route, the whole journey coincides here and there with what is known, perhaps romantically, as the Pilgrims' Way, as many of the road names will tell you. But which pilgrims, and did they truly progress along this way? Chaucer's pilgrims, of course, travelled from London to Canterbury so, despite a fanciful sign near Guildford, it seems more likely that his travellers followed the line of the A2. In fact, many believe that the Pilgrims' Way did not acquire its appellation until the 1860s, when an Ordnance Survey officer decided that the route should be so-called. Prior to that, local historians have been unable to unearth any such designation.

On the other hand, it seems possible that men and women might have travelled from what was formerly the secular capital of the ancient kingdom of Wessex, Winchester, to England's spiritual centre, Canterbury, following the martyrdom of Thomas à Becket in 1170. In medieval Europe, the holiness and pastoral powers of a canonised churchman did not end with his death, and the sight or touch of a saint's remains was held to be a cure for disorders of the soul and thereby for those of the body. What better route could such a pilgrim choose than one that had probably been in use for thousands of years, perhaps ever since migrating animals first made their way from east to west, journeying in a direction that avoided the densest forests of the ridge tops as well as the marshy hollows of the Weald?

Like the Ridgeway, between Avebury in Wiltshire and Ivinghoe Beacon in Buckinghamshire, the various routes along the line of the North Downs may well form part of the network of some of the oldest 'roads' in Europe, mentioned in Anglo-Saxon charters. Some believe that there were actually two east–west routes, one along the ridge top used in more primitive times and the other, lower down and with fewer steep gradients, used in more settled times for travellers with pack animals. It has been suggested that the line of the North Downs was used as part of a trading link, established after the retreat of the ice some 10,000 years ago, between the peoples of Surrey and Kent and the Isle of Portland where chert, preferred to flint for tool-making, was to be found. But perhaps, as J. R. L. Anderson claims for the Ridgeway, paths along the North Downs first came into use at least 250,000 years ago when Palaeolithic, pre-Ice Age hunters climbed on to the hills to find their quarry.

Certainly, until perhaps 5,000 years ago, when Britain was finally separated from what is now continental Europe by the English Channel and the Straits of Dover, people from western and northern Europe may have gained access to central England via these routes. By this time, the glaciers from the last of the Ice Age had long since melted and the climate had improved. Stone Age humans would, once again, have spread throughout this part of Britain.

Whether this is the case, it seems reasonable to suppose that green roads along the North Downs were used for cattle droving and for travelling long distances on foot or horseback, in much the same way as the Ridgeway was, to avoid natural hazards and possibly even brigands who could more easily conceal themselves in the tangled forests below. These trackways along the North Downs may have enjoyed a revival during the 18th century when the system of turnpike roads was in being.

It is largely in this century that the present system of main, trunk and motorway roads has come into being, with some

While it is the Surrey end of the National Trail that is most extensively wooded

following the lines of older routes, such as Roman roads. With the coming of the new means of communication, the old ways have fallen into disuse, except as convenient access roads for farmers or as footpaths and rights of way for today's nomads – pleasure walkers, horseriders and cyclists. While you journey along the North Downs you might muse upon previous travellers who have passed that way but, from time to time, as you pass close to busy trunk roads or cross roaring motorways, you are brought back with a jolt to the 20th century.

Today, responsibility for managing the North Downs Way National Trail lies with the county councils of Kent and Surrey and is coordinated by an officer who is partly funded by the Countryside Commission.

there is delightful broad-leaved woodland in Kent, too.

Practical advice

Walking, cycling or riding a horse on the North Downs Way do not require the same precautions as pursuing these activities on a mountain in Wales or Scotland. The weather is rarely very severe; it is hard to get seriously lost; the going underfoot is not dangerous and is, at worst, wet and rutted; and you are seldom far from help should it be needed. On the other hand, there is no point in making life difficult for yourself – after all, pleasure, not risk or discomfort, is likely to be your incentive for strolling on the Way. A few simple precautions should enhance your enjoyment of the route. Remember that, though this may be a walk in the 'soft South', you face some lung-testing climbs, such as the ascent of Box Hill.

If you are walking, the single most important piece of equipment to get right is footwear. Almost everyone who ever sets foot to footpath has a different view on what it is best to wear on the feet, but one thing is certain: unless you usually live in them, you do not need foot-dragging heavy mountain boots here. For short walks, especially during winter or spring when parts of the way might be very boggy, wellington boots are as good as anything. But I would not advise wearing 'wellies' for more than a mile or two. Some people prefer to be as lightly shod as possible, almost regardless of going or weather; if you are one of them, then trainers are probably your best bet, but remember that wet feet can soon become sore and very cold. For me the best compromise is a pair of modern lightweight walking boots or shoes. These come in a variety of designs, materials and qualities, reflected in the price you pay. There are those who claim that you must always wear top-quality leather boots for comfort, breathability and reasonable proof against the wet, while others say that you cannot beat fabric boots for comfort and light weight but accept that these boots do not keep out water for long. Even the soles of boots range in thickness, weight, stiffness and tread pattern. The best bet is to go to a reputable outdoor clothing stockist for advice or, better still, read the outdoor magazines for expert reviews.

Then, of course, there are socks. I know diehards who maintain that you must only ever wear three pairs of thick woollen socks under your boots. I stopped doing that years ago and replaced them with a single pair of loop-stitch socks, although in winter I might wear an extra pair of woollen socks underneath. In any case, if you are out for the day or longer, always carry a spare pair. There is little worse than squelching mile after mile in wet or sweaty socks. Nowadays, even socks have been given the technologists' treatment and there are various kinds of so-called 'supersocks' available – at a price.

Clothing, too, has come a long way since the mandatory tweeds and cords for the great outdoors, but again it is up to you to find out what suits you best. For three seasons of the year, a pair of polycotton walking trousers, a shirt, a spare sweater or thermofleece garment and a waterproof (preferably breathable) are all that you really need. In winter, extra warm clothing, a hat and gloves are a good idea; the downs can be quite exposed to winter winds, especially near the coast and where the great storm of 1987 demolished old woodland.

If I am out for the day or longer, I usually carry a small first-aid kit containing some painkillers, plasters, some 'moleskin', 'animal wool', or chiropodist's felt, a tube of antiseptic cream, and, during the season, some antihistamine cream. If you do sometimes fall foul to the dreaded blister, a modern 'blister-repair kit', with its special ingredient of 'second skin', can provide near-blissful relief to sore feet. On longer trips, I might also include a triangular bandage, a crêpe bandage and some wound dressings. There is no point, however, in weighing yourself down with these if you do not know how to use them, and they are certainly not essential.

It is rare on the North Downs Way not to be able to find refreshment during the day; a recent survey identified nearly 300 pubs and 200 shops within a couple of miles of the Trail, ignoring those in the main settlements. But it is still a good idea to carry a drink with you and some high-energy food in case of emergency.

This guide book, together with the waymarks that you will find along the whole length of the path, should enable you to follow the route without any other assistance although, from time to time, signs do get vandalised. The waymarking along the North Downs Way is good, and you should be able to follow quite easily the finger-posts, waymark signs and reassuring white acorns. In Surrey you will find that the directional fingers are made from traditional routed wood backed up with reassuring and clear coloured disks. In Kent the wooden signs are replaced by metal ones, again backed up by disks, and, in places, you will still find some of the old, concrete, low-level signposts.

You do not require one, but it can be very satisfying to carry a compass with you and know how to use it. If nothing else, it might enable you more easily to identify features off the track and, in any case, it is useful to be able to practise the use of map and compass when you know where you are.

You will need a rucksack. Buy the best that you can afford. Again, read the magazines, take advice, and try several types for comfort (especially with some weight in it) and access to its various pockets and compartments. It is very frustrating to have to undo lots of buckles, strings and zips and then empty the whole thing to find your 'blister-repair kit' when your feet are sore and you are hopping around with one boot on and one off. Remember that, even if you treat the seams with a sealing compound, rucksacks are rarely completely waterproof and it is sensible to contain most of your belongings inside plastic bags within the rucksack. And do not forget to keep the weight down!

It is possible to find places to camp at intervals along the route although, unless you are on an official camp site where you will need to check in anyway, you should always seek permission to do so. There is a very wide variety of 'high-tech' and 'not-so-high-tech' lightweight tents to choose from. But, if you camp, you will need a bigger rucksack to cope with tent and sleeping bag. It is perfectly possible to walk the whole route making use of the seven youth hostels and 200 or so guest houses, inns and hotels sited on or near the route so that you do not have to carry so much with you. You will find information about accommodation on page 163.

In places, horseriders and cyclists will find the going heavy after wet weather. Deep sand on some parts of the route may be comfortable going for the hoof, but even the thick tyres of all-terrain bikes will sink to the rims. And where the way is chalky, waterlogged ruts pose problems to the thoroughbred and the bicycle in almost equal measure. In a dry summer, the ruts set rock hard and flints might puncture feet or tyres, so be sure to take precautionary measures and repair kits.

Characteristic features of Kent are the oast houses – drying kilns for the newly picked hops.

PART TWO

NORTH DOWNS WAY

1 Farnham to Guildford

through Puttenham
11 miles (17.7 km)

To start your walk along the North Downs Way, turn left out of Farnham railway station entrance, go down the hill towards the A31, and turn right at the traffic lights on to the main road. There is a carved post here marking the start of the Trail, though the traffic does not encourage you to pause and admire it. You soon come to a metalled lane to the right, signposted North Downs Way. Continue walking along the shady, tree-lined lane. At the T-junction with another lane, turn right as indicated. If you listen, and are fortunate, you may hear a King-fisher's whistle at the point where the metalled lane changes to gravel. Noise from the A31 continues to intrude upon the walk, although it does not quite drown the bird song as you walk among the beech, oak and rowan trees, and you soon approach the River Wey **1** which, with its meadows, make an attractive buffer between walker and the A31.

Walk along the pleasant lane beside the River Wey. At The Kiln, turn right away from the river along the footpath and go under the Victorian brick railway bridge.

You are now walking along a pleasant woodland-edge path with broad water meadows to the left. As you reach the end of the meadows and approach some woodland, look out for the wooden finger-post where you bear left along the North Downs Way round the woodland. Shortly afterwards watch for a turning to the right over a stile, where there is one of the Countryside Commission's white acorn markers on the gatepost. These acorn markers will guide you along the whole National Trail. You are now on a grassy track through the fields with mature trees all around.

After 100 yards (90 metres) or so, climb another stile and the path now continues beside a line of oak trees. In about another 100 yards, cross a stile and you emerge on to a road where you turn left. When you come to a turning on the left, follow a North Downs Way finger-post pointing left around the corner opposite a post box. Moor Park Lane crosses the river by a little bridge. You now walk between a lime hedge and a brick wall, approaching a crossroads. Walk on up the hill to Compton Way, passing Campana International College and Flower School **2** on the right.

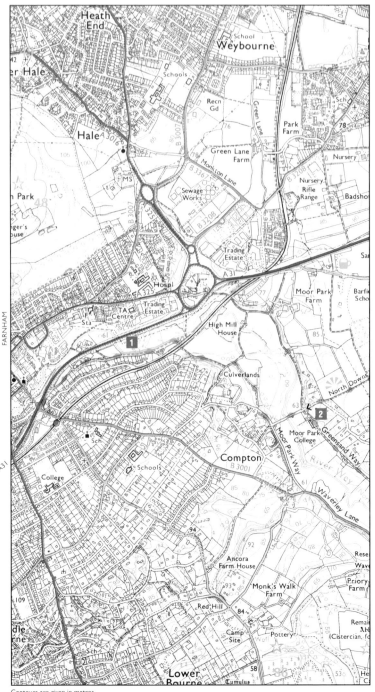

Contours are given in metres
The vertical interval is 5m

29

At the top of the hill, where the road bends to the right, look out for the finger-post which directs you straight ahead on to a footpath again. This is Wey Hanger – 'hanger' being an Old English word for a wood on the edge of a steep hill.

Go over another stile on your right and walk along the left-hand side of the field. From here there are good views over Farnham to the left. This is pleasant walking country through Moor Park, and it is good to be well away from the town. Cross a stile and follow the well-worn track through mixed woodland, passing the sand workings on the left. Cross another broad track and continue straight onwards between two wire fences. Continue down a bank, and turn right. You are now walking along a broad, slightly sunken track where the going underfoot is sandy.

At the next finger-post turn left and pass by an extensive modern bungalow on the right-hand side of the track. You are now walking through the wood beside a road to your right. You will pass more houses on your left before the track becomes a metalled lane and arrives at a road, where you should turn left. Go down the hill a little, cross the road, and turn right after about 20 yards (18 metres). You are now on another fence-lined woodland track, only to emerge on to another road after about 50 yards (45 metres); turn right again, walk along the road, passing an impressive modern brick house on the right, a golf driving range on the left and Sandy Farm.

Next pass Farnham Golf Club and, just past the clubhouse, turn left. After about 400 yards (365 metres), where the road bends to the left, turn right and climb over another stile. You are now walking around the edge of another part of the golf course, once again on a well-defined path with a beech hedge on the left. The path now takes you into the trees beside a chain-link fence on your left.

Cross the road and continue straight along the track. After a short distance on this gravel track pass through a fence. Now you have open fields to the right. The going underfoot on this stretch of the Trail is very sandy indeed and you could easily be walking on a beach. In early summer it is a hive of wildlife activity, with squirrels and rabbits and snatches of bird song all around. By a small collection of conifer trees, look out for the finger-post taking you over a rustic stile to the right **A**. In about 50 yards (45 metres), you come to another stile, where you turn right and follow the path as it turns left, along the right side of a hedge.

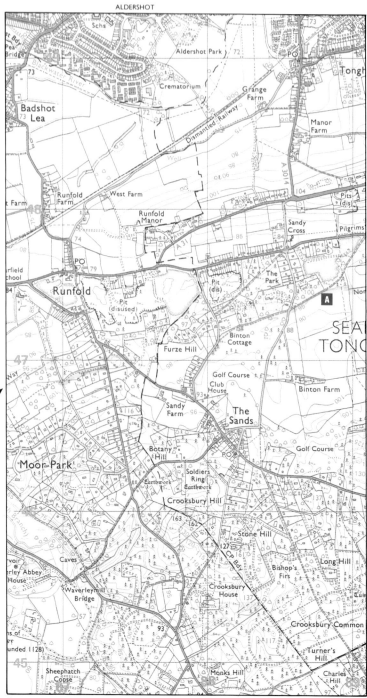

Contours are given in metres
The vertical interval is 5m

31

At the end of the field, through a gap in the hedge, cross another sandy, sunken lane and continue straight on along the edge of the field, again with the hedge to your left. You soon arrive at the road in front of a large white house with a smaller stone-built house in front of it. Turn right and immediately left, going over the stile. After 200 yards (180 metres) you turn left again and then go over another stile. There is an open field to your left and woodland to the right. In about 50 yards (45 metres) you cross a stile, and turn immediately right to walk along the left-hand edge of a piece of woodland, with the hill falling away to the left. There are now pleasant views across the valley, but the tranquillity of the scene is marred a little by the distant roar of traffic on the Hog's Back road to your left.

Go over a stile and into another patch of woodland. Drop down a little and enter an area of recently planted trees. Where the newish plantation comes to an end, the track bears to the right and you pass by another stile to walk on a sunken woodland track as it descends. You soon arrive at a narrow private road where you turn left. Go through a gate by a red-brick bungalow with the date 1893 on its chimney and turn right on to

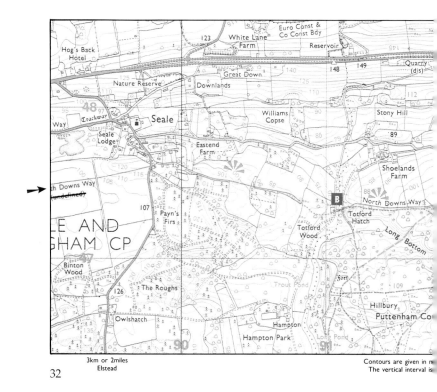

3km or 2miles
Elstead

Contours are given in m
The vertical interval is

a woodland lane **B**. Cross the little stream and go on up the sandy lane at the edge of Puttenham Common; this continues upwards.

As you near the top of the rise, before reaching a red-brick house, the path forks and your way is to the left. At the sign, turn left. There are good views across the valley to the Hog's Back on your left and the wild honeysuckle is abundant here. The sunken track now winds and undulates through the woodland, then emerges from the narrow track to arrive at a metalled drive to Stable Cottage. Continue straight ahead down another sunken lane. At the T-junction in the lanes, bear leftish, more or less straight on, and, at the next angled T-junction by the post office, turn right into The Street at Puttenham – again this is effectively straight on. Go on through the main street of Puttenham towards the rather odd-looking church of St John the Baptist **3**. Pass the church and, at the T-junction with the B3000, you turn right, signposted towards Compton and Godalming.

Opposite a restaurant, and next to Puttenham Golf Club, turn left. This is a public bridleway which, at first, is partly

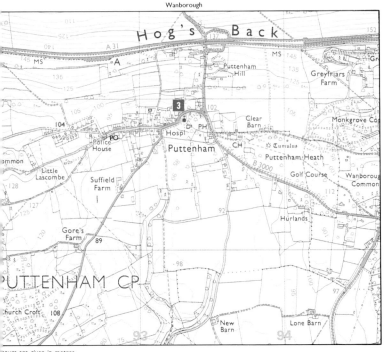

metalled. Where the metalled lane forks, keep to the right and, by a row of posts marking the edge of the golf course, continue straight on down the gravel track. Follow the drive straight on downhill, keeping some houses to your left. At a staggered crossroads in the path **C**, continue straight on, bearing a little left. As you emerge from the woodland, pass beneath the busy A3 on a metalled lane – note that the slipway bridge is marked with wooden crosses, apparently to mark the Pilgrims' Way **4**. At the T-junction, turn left towards the Watts Gallery **5** (see page 38) and, unless you are visiting the gallery, or the excellent teashop, turn right on to another sandy lane.

The path becomes a sunken lane into some woodland and goes uphill. At a crossing of paths, continue straight on up the hill. This is Loseley Estate's nature reserve **6** and is pleasant woodland with some overgrown and unmanaged old coppice. Descending the hill through the woods, the path is really very deep sand. Where the track forks, take the public footpath to the left and then turn immediately right **D** where there is a rather concealed finger-post.

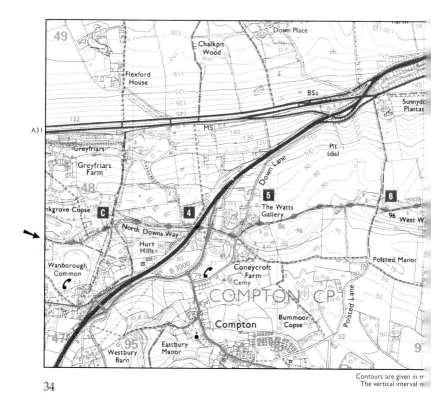

Contours are given in m
The vertical interval is

At a T-junction with a partly surfaced lane turn left and then, in about 30 yards (27 metres), turn right on to Piccard's Farm private road. You soon arrive at the houses that mark the outskirts of Guildford. Emerging on to the road, you turn left and then, as you come out of Sandy Lane on to the A road opposite Ye Olde Ship Inn, turn right and immediately left into Ferry Lane opposite the College of Law. This path descends steeply, crossing the railway line. Go through a tree arch, pass a little bower with a rocky seat and pixie's bridge, and continue down towards the River Wey once more. Turn right and cross the river using the wooden footbridge. After this turn left and then right by a marker post. Cross the open space of Shalford Park and you soon arrive at the busy A281 to the south of Guildford. From here there is a regular bus service into the city or it would take you about fifteen minutes to walk to the centre, where you will find all the usual facilities of a large town. Alternatively, instead of crossing the bridge and the park, it is possible to follow the west bank of the Wey towards Guildford.

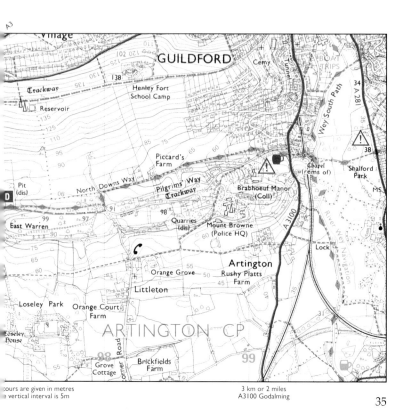

The River Wey near Guildford (see page 35) is, understandably, popular with

Farnham

Your journey to the sea may begin at Farnham and, eager to get under way, it is all too tempting not to spare the time to take a closer look at your starting point, especially if you have arrived by train on the 'wrong' side of the Farnham bypass. Most visitors to Farnham will not fail to be struck by the Georgian elegance of Castle Street, leading up to Farnham Castle, where the Norman keep, kitchens and chapel still survive. But Castle Street predates the 18th century and was originally designed to be wide enough to hold fairs and markets. It is only the façades of the houses that give the street its Georgian appearance – all except the Windsor Almshouses, which have retained their early 17th century character.

visitors and residents alike, particularly at weekends and on bank holidays.

Like so many towns in England, Farnham's prosperity in the Middle Ages came from the cloth trade but, in the 18th century, it was to a crop that we more usually associate with Kent that the town owed its wealth – the humble hop. Fortunes were made and lost by growing hops and from brewing and, in an age when there are probably less than 200 commercial breweries in the country, it is astonishing to learn that a small town like Farnham once had five of its own. It was from hops and from brewing, therefore, that local worthies made enough money to add the beautifully proportioned frontages, sash windows and classical entrances to some of the existing buildings.

Such street names as Red Lion Lane or Lion and Lamb Yard are evidence of the town's brewery history, and one of the buildings worth examining is The Maltings on Red Lion Lane.

In fact, it began life as a tannery in the 18th century, changed its trade to brewing in the 19th, and then, in 1850, began to be used for malting barley. And just across the road is the house where the politician and journalist, William Cobbett, was born in 1763. He was a traveller, too, and is probably best known for his outspoken and very personal chronicle of eighteenth century life, *Rural Rides*. Appropriately, the building is now the William Cobbett public house.

Some of the other buildings worth looking at are Tanyard House near The Maltings, Vernon House, which is now the public library on West Street, Sandford House and Willmer House on the other side of West Street, and the mainly 15th century church of St Andrew standing by the River Wey, where Cobbett's tomb is to be found opposite the porch.

Farnham's origins are much older even than its Norman castle, which was built by a grandson of William I, Henri de Blois. There is evidence that Palaeolithic people occupied the site, and certainly the Romans were here for 400 years after their invasion of England in the 1st century. Like that of other places, such as Fareham or Ferneham, the name comes from Saxon words meaning, roughly, 'ferny meadow'. In the late 7th century, a Saxon ruler of the kingdom of Wessex, Caedwalla, handed Farnham lock, stock and barrel to the Christian church as a gift and as a site for a monastery, no remains of which now survive.

The Watts Gallery, Compton

The English artist, George Frederic Watts (1817–1904) first came to Compton with his second wife in 1886. They holidayed with friends during the autumn and winter of that year, mainly to escape the fogs of London, where they had a house in Kensington. The Watts liked rural Surrey so much that, in 1891, they built the house 'Limnerslease' about half a mile (800 metres) to the west of Compton and right beside what is now the route of the North Downs Way.

Watts had begun his career as a sculptor studying under Behnes. He won a prize for the decoration of the Houses of Parliament and, in 1887, began a series of portraits of famous men of the day, in which he attempted not only to paint their physical appearance but also to convey their personalities. It was a collection of his portraits that Watts presented to the National Gallery in 1896, and he also donated other paintings to the Tate.

Watts's wife firmly believed that her husband was the world's greatest living artist, and many others thought him to be England's foremost painter of the age. Whatever inspired the idea, Watts decided that he should preserve and exhibit those pictures that remained in his possession, and the concept of the Watts Gallery duly came into being. The gallery **5** was designed by a friend, Christopher Turnor, and the foundation stone was laid by the artist himself in the grounds of his Surrey house in 1903, when Watts was 86 years old.

A year later Watts died and his wife came to live permanently at their house near Compton, where she remained until her death in 1938. Today, the gallery is open free to the public throughout the year, apart from Good Friday, Christmas Eve and Christmas Day. There is a tea shop in the grounds so that, even for those without an artistic bent, the Watts Gallery could offer refreshment to weary travellers. If there is time, the Watts chapel nearby is also well worth a visit.

In its curious mixture of architectural styles, the Watts memorial temple is an extraordinary edifice, built partly by local craftsmen.

2 Guildford to the Mole Valley and the A24

via Newlands Corner and Ranmore Common
13 miles (21 km)

If you have stopped overnight in Guildford, make your way back along the A281 to the point where the North Downs Way emerges from Shalford Park. Cross the busy A281 and continue on to Pilgrims' Way directly ahead. Just beyond the line of tall lime trees, bear right along a partly metalled driveway then, by the white-painted Chantry Cottage, follow the lane to the left, with Chantries woods on your right. Continue straight on through the woods near Whinny Hill where the path is crossed by another track.

You soon arrive at the minor road where you turn left and then immediately right by the 30 mph restriction sign. Follow the broad sandy lane through the woods, passing Southern Way House and entering an open clearing for a short distance. This is the Surrey County Council's Open Space of St Martha's Hill. Continue, following the steep footpath to the top of St Martha's Hill **7**. This is an airy spot with fine views all around.

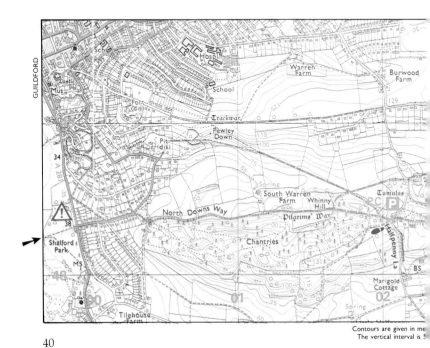

Contours are given in me
The vertical interval is !

With the church (see page 49) to your right, continue along the track. As you reach the east-facing scarp slope, keep the viewing rail to your right and descend the hill on the main sandy track. Partway down the hill, look out for the acorn post **A** indicating that your way forks to the left a little. This is the junction with the Downslink Path.

Just before reaching White Lane, turn left and immediately right and into the woods again. This is a narrow woodland track that runs parallel to the road for a short distance, and you pass White Lane Farm before bearing left and starting to climb between a hedge-lined fence on the left and woods on the right. Turn right at the end of the path, go down some concrete steps, and cross the road on to another path, soon forking right. Emerge into the fields and follow the path, continuing to climb.

There are various routes across the Albury Downs, but the official Way keeps to the left along the line of the trees and there are lovely views all around. Simply walk towards the Visitors' Centre at the popular beauty spot of Newlands Corner **8**, where there is a car park and refreshments. Between the car park and the downslope trees, look out for the finger-post **B**. Cross the road, aiming a little to the right and into the woodlands once more. (Alternative routes for crossing the A25 are being looked

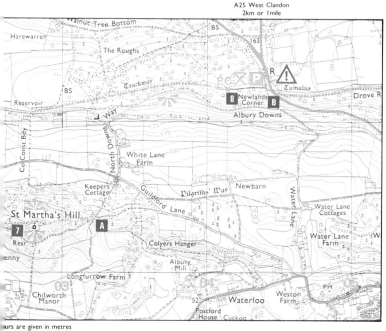

urs are given in metres
vertical interval is 5m

at, so follow the waymarking carefully at this point.) The line of the track and your route is clear.

After a mile and half (2.5 km), at West Hanger car park, where there are picnic tables, you cross the lane and continue straight on along the path through the woodland. You soon come to a road again, where you turn right and immediately left to follow the track down towards Hollister Farm. Once there, keep left, walk past the stables and go through an acorn-marked gate.

At a crossing of paths where there is an odd concrete circular construction, a relic of the Canadian army's presence in World War II, your way is more or less straight on **D**. You are now walking along a partly tarmacked forest lane and, where this lane crosses other tracks, continue straight ahead along what is clearly the main path. At another junction, where there is another of these strange concrete tanks, keep going straight ahead. Although it is not obvious, your legs might tell you you are now on a slight upward incline.

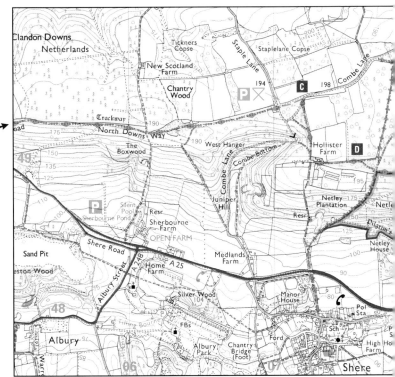

Contours are given in m
The vertical interval is

Just over half a mile (1 km) after you have passed Gravelhill Gate, where the track forks, do not follow the more obvious way straight on, but fork right to get to a wooden finger-post, which takes you hard right through a gate and down a grassy drove much enjoyed by rabbits.

The drove becomes a pleasant woodland track where fine views break through the trees on your right. At a gate do not go through but fork left up the hill. On reaching the rutted lane, turn left, and after 50 yards (45 metres) turn right onto the grassy path again. Note how the clay, with flints and rather acid soils capping the chalk, provides habitat for birch and gorse scrub. Cross the bridleway into Blatchford Down named after one of the founding members of the Long Distance Walkers Association. Cross Beggars Lane **9** through two kissing gates and take time to admire the view through the gaps created by the 1987 storm. A brick bunker is passed about 200 yards (180 metres) into the field. Go through the gateway into White Down Lease. A finger-post is situated at a crossing of paths **E**, indicat-

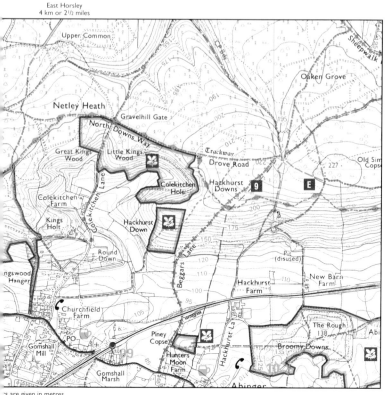

's are given in metres
rtical interval is 5m

ing a slight climb uphill to the left past another pillbox. Turn sharply right with the path to go down a sunken lane towards the road, then turn right down the road for about 5 yards before turning left up a chalky track.

You are now heading north-east along a track through the woods; you pass another two brick pill boxes and a kissing gate and there are still good views along this section of the route. This is excellent chalk grassland, quilted into the patchy woodland, typical of the downs landscape. Much of this land is owned by the National Trust, whose policy is to graze the downs in order to maintain the variety and value of the grassland. Since the storm of 1987 more downland has been exposed and, recognising the comparative rarity of such habitat in Britain, the Trust is keen to preserve the grassland, and the viewpoints it provides, against the encroaching scrub. In summer this area is alive with butterflies.

Cross another stile, go down into a sunken lane, turn left, and pass through the hunting gate, heading uphill once again, and pass by yet another brick pillbox. Look out for an acorn

From the vantage point of Ranmore Common, near Dorking, the scene is one extolled by lovers of the southern English countryside.

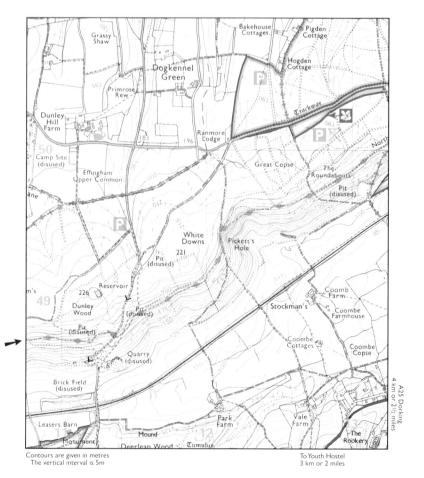

Contours are given in metres
The vertical interval is 5m

To Youth Hostel
3 km or 2 miles

post taking you right on to a narrower woodland track, and the scarp slope to your right drops away very steeply. The path now follows the contour and it is all too easy to stumble over exposed tree roots. Where large trees have fallen across the path, convenient cuts allow you to pass.

Continue straight on through the woods for some time, the railway line running at the foot of the scarp provides the only occasional reminder of civilisation. There are clear views of Dorking. As I walked along this almost arrow-straight path through the woods I was accompanied by the melodic piping and warbling of a male blackbird – nothing rare, but just as sweet for all that.

Just before 'Steerfield', named after the other founding member of the LDWA, the track forks, take the right-hand fork, aiming towards the church tower of Ranmore Common, and go across the grassy meadow. In the meadow, take the right-hand of the two tracks, aiming a little to the right of the church and trees.

At the two-way finger-post, bear left, then go through two gates, fork right, and aim for the road. Where the road from Ranmore joins the main road at a T-junction, continue straight on towards Ranmore Common, signposted to Bookham and Westhumble. Pass by the church of St Barnabas at Ranmore **10**, known as The Church on the North Downs Way. The church was built by Sir George Gilbert Scott in 1860 for Lord Ashcombe, son of the great Victorian builder, Thomas Cubitt.

Where the road turns sharply to the left **F**, carry straight on for a few yards along the lane that states it is a 'Private Drive' and then turn right into the estate with its deer fences. At a

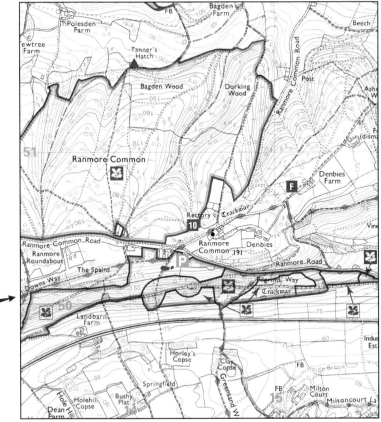

Contours are given in metres
The vertical interval is 5m

three-way finger-post turn left and then continue to the right, and pass through the forbidding-looking deer gates. On the south-facing slope there is the famous Denbies vineyard.

Pass through another set of deer gates and you will be able to see the densely wooded summit of Boxhill. The gravel lane continues to follow the contour of the hill for a while. Cross a gravelled forest road and continue straight on, passing one track to the right. At a fork, bear right, and you are now descending a little more quickly towards the road. Go through a diamond-bar gate and under a gloomy, Victorian railway bridge. You emerge on to the busy dual carriageway of the A24 (there is an underpass a quarter of a mile/400 metres to the north). Dorking lies a couple of miles south, along the A24 to your right, and offers most facilities. There is a pub in Westhumble, just to the north, and, nearby, the Burford Bridge Hotel.

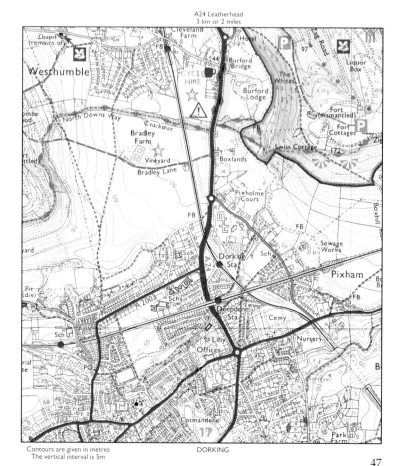

Contours are given in metres
The vertical interval is 5m

DORKING

A circular walk from the St Martha's Hill car park

3½ miles (5.2 km)

This is an attractive walk, combining good views across the Weald with relatively flat, easy walking; the route is mostly sheltered by the woodland on the sandy ridge. From the car park, walk back to Halfpenny Lane and turn left, passing Southernway Cottage. Turn right to enter Chantries Woods by the steel barrier. Where the track divides, fork left and walk on until you reach the toilets. There is a good view from here, just off the path, but worth exploring. Continue on through the woods on the main track to a large oak tree with a circular bench. Bear right, down the hill, and the edge of the wood will soon become apparent. Turn right at another seat and follow the path, with the field on the left, down to the North Downs Way.

At the crossroads, continue straight on the broad track. Notice Pewley Down on the left as the track bears to the right before reaching the lane again. There is an attractive, hand-painted panel in this section, depicting some of the wildlife which can be found in the area.

Cross the road and go through the farmyard. Carry on for just over three-quarters of a mile (1.3 km) until you reach the corner of Guildford Lane by Keepers Cottage. Turn right on to the North Downs Way, which heads uphill along sandy tracks more suitable for horses' hooves than walkers' boots. Nearing the top of the hill bear right towards the church of St Martha's

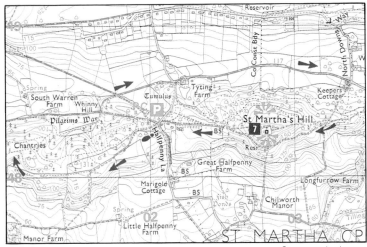

Contours are given in metres
The vertical interval is 5m

Hill. This is an airy spot and there are fine views all around. Keeping the church to your left, follow the clear track downhill among the conifers. At a clearing, fork right to cross a field and follow the path back to the car park.

Like any circular walk, this one can be tackled in either direction, but it seems to make sense to retain its climax, the heights of St Martha's Hill **7**, until near the end.

The church of St Martha on the Hill

St Martha's Hill, a mile or two to the east of Guildford, reaches a height of 573 feet (almost 175 metres) above sea level and, it is claimed, it is possible to see into eight counties from its summit. Four remaining earth circles on the hill are evidence, local archaeologists believe, that it was a sacred site as far back as the Bronze Age. Later reference to 'Marterhill' suggests that St Martha's Hill was being used by pagans for burning the Christian missionaries of St Augustine at the beginning of the 7th century AD.

Parts of the present church, such as the transepts and crossing, were probably built in about the year AD 1200, but it seems that there must have been a church on the same site for nearly 200 years before that, following its conversion from a site for '. . . the worship of devils to the service of the one true God'. While some people still claim that 'Martha' is simply a corruption of the word 'martyr', it is a more popularly held view that the church was dedicated to St Martha of Bethany, the sister of Mary Magdalene, at the time of the Norman Conquest and, even in 12th and 13th century documents, it was referred to as *Ecclesia Sanctae Marthae*.

If, in medieval times, pilgrims did follow the route from Winchester to Canterbury to seek out the place of martyrdom of St Thomas, then it seems likely that St Martha's Church may well have been among the holy places *en route* where they would have worshipped. But St Martha's has itself been an object of pilgrimage, at least since 1463 when Bishop Waynflete of Winchester encouraged people that '. . . if being truly penitent, contrite, and confessed of their sins, they should come to the chapel dedicated to Saint Martha the Virgin . . . for the sake of devotion, prayer, pilgrimage, or offering . . .' And even today pilgrims still come to pray at the parish church.

On Surrey County Council's Open Space of St Martha's Hill is perched the 13th century church dedicated to St Martha of Bethany.

A CIRCULAR WALK ON RANMORE COMMON
4 miles (6.4 km)

This attractive walk forms a loop around much of the common land owned by the National Trust. The Polesden Lacey estate a short distance away is well worth a visit. From the car parking area near the fork in the Ranmore Common Road, where there are signposts to Bookham and Westhumble, cross the road and turn left along the grassy verge as far as Rose Cottage. Take the public bridleway on the right into the woods, continuing on this main track until you emerge into a field. Cross the field, passing to the right of Bagden Farm, and continue on until you reach the road, Chapel Lane. Turn right and carry on down the road, passing Olde Dene before taking the first road to the right signed to Ranmore Common. After about 140 yards (130 metres), at the end of a line of cottages, turn left through a farm gate.

Keeping the open field on your right, cross a stile and walk on, with a wood on your right, to reach a second stile, which leads into a field. Follow the line of the telegraph posts to a final stile which leads into the drive for Ashleigh Grange. Turn right and then keep left into the Dentries Estate. When you come to the North Downs Way, turn right. Follow the North Downs Way signs until you reach Ranmore Common Road again at a sharp corner. Continue on past the flint-built church to St Barnabas at Ranmore **10** until you get to the junction. Turn right and head back to the car park.

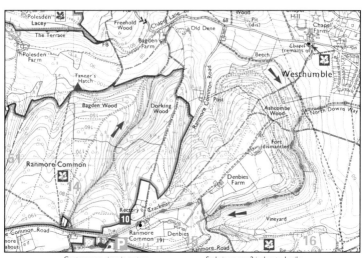

Contours are given in metres
The vertical interval is 5m

Scale is approx 2 inches to 1 mile

3 The Mole Valley to Merstham

over Box Hill and Reigate Hill
10 miles (16.1 km)

If you have broken your journey at Dorking or Burford Bridge Hotel, simply make your way back along the A24 towards Box Hill Country Park. You now need to cross the busy A24, so turn left and continue for about a quarter of a mile (400 metres) northwards towards Westhumble Street, where there is an underpass. Returning along the other side of the road you will come, almost opposite the point where you emerged from the Denbies Estate, to the car park at the National Trust's Stepping Stones site **A**. Here you turn left and follow the path to the River Mole. You can cross by the stepping stones, to the right **11** or you can take the lefthand path to the bridge, both options lead to a track on the other bank.

After a short stretch of gravel track, the path begins to ascend very steeply, using steps cut in the side of the hill. After a rather

The stepping stones across the River Mole are easy enough for all but the most unsteady to negotiate, except at times of very high water.

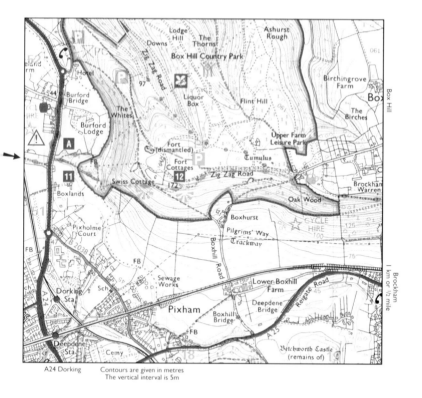

A24 Dorking   Contours are given in metres
The vertical interval is 5m

breathless climb, through a yew wood you will find yourself almost at the top of Box Hill itself (see page 58) and there are splendid views across the Weald towards the South Downs. You soon reach the triangulation pillar **12** and a viewing platform, erected in 'grateful remembrance' of the man who gave Box Hill to the nation. The Visitor Centre and café, well worth a visit, are a few hundred yards away at the very top of the hill.

You are now just below the road. Continue straight on along the southern edge of the ridge. Look out for a marker post taking you off the main track along the ridge, to the left and uphill. Follow the markers into the woods near the road and then continue onwards, negotiating various tracks and gullies. Then turn left and up some steps along the hillside again. By a gate, turn right once again on to a more even path. Go down some steps with a wooden bannister which lead downwards through the woods. On reaching the bottom, you turn left and uphill. This is another steep climb and should be tackled with caution as the chalk can become very slippery when wet.

At the fork, the track branches and your way is the narrower path to the right. Shortly after the little memorial to 'Quick, An English Thoroughbred 26.9.36–22.10.44' **13**, walk down some wooden steps and turn right at the finger-post.

The path comes off the bank and into the ditch beside it. Follow the path as it winds its way downwards and continue through the quarry area, noting the lime-kiln to your right, a survivor in this ever-changing landscape. You will then come to a finger-post, where you turn right. Cross the chalky track **B** between the two branches of the quarry working and continue on between two lines of fencing. Cross another gated track and soon you arrive at the turning area of a cul-de-sac road, with a line of houses on the left. Where the unmetalled part of the road meets broken tarmac, and where you can see Combe Cottages, look out for the finger-post taking you straight ahead and bearing a little to the right. You soon emerge from The Combe on to Pebblehill Road, and you turn left **C** up the road.

Pass the white-painted, timber-framed, almost Tudor-looking Cranmer Cottage, with its eagle on the gatepost and, just by a house on the left, look out for a 'Footway' sign on the left.

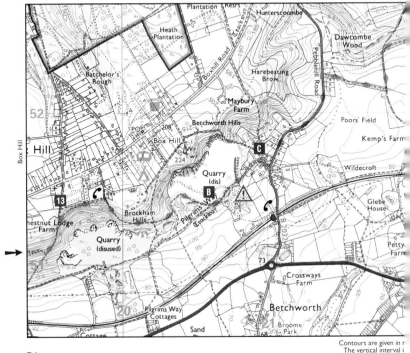

Contours are given in r
The vertical interval i

The footway emerges on to the noisy road again and you are obliged to cross to the other side. Just past a house called Pebbledown, go right and away from the road. You soon arrive at a gated stile leading into a field, then head left. You must go through an iron gate to follow a path up the side of the field with a fence on your left. Walk up the hill and into the woods. At a fork in the paths, aim right and then, by some tall yew trees, join another path turning right and head downhill on a broad track. You will soon pass another small old quarry working, and, when you come to a finger-post, you turn left, heading uphill.

Where one track comes in behind you and the track splits immediately afterwards, fork left. Continue straight on, following the edge of the woods round the foot of Juniper Hill but at a crossroads in the tracks turn left and head uphill on a steep, chalky track on to the National Trust property of Colley Hill **14**. The track veers to the left partway up the hill. When you reach the top of the hill you emerge on to a narrow metalled lane where you turn right. Go along the lane for about 10 yards (9 metres) and turn right.

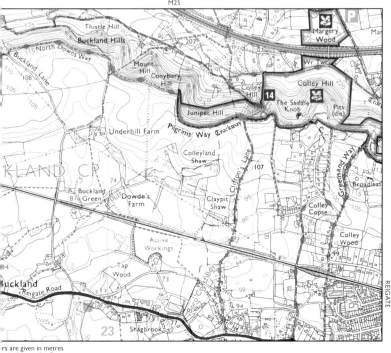

rs are given in metres
ertical interval is 5m

Continue straight on towards what looks like a miniature Georgian pavilion **15**. It is a little roofed seating area with a blue ceiling picked out by gold stars and was presented to the Corporation of the Borough of Reigate for the benefit of the public by Lieutenant-Colonel Robert William Inglis in 1909. From here there are splendid views along the North Downs, and across Reigate and the Weald to the South Downs.

The Way now bears left along the lane and leads you to a gate at a water storage tank, the track becomes tarmacadamed. Continue along the track and pass by Reigate Fort. This is followed by a rather more mundane, if more useful, establishment, the Hilltop Holiday Home for Cats! The lane descends towards the noise of passing traffic, and soon you arrive at a white-painted footbridge that crosses the A217, which, to the south, leads directly into Reigate.

After crossing the bridge, you arrive at a car park, where there are toilets and refreshment facilities. Follow the finger-posts and acorn markers through the National Trust site, turning right by the cottages at the bottom into Gatton Park school grounds **16**. Keep left, passing the various buildings, including the comparatively modern Assembly Hall. The original house, built by Lord Monson in 1830, was burnt down in 1934 but the

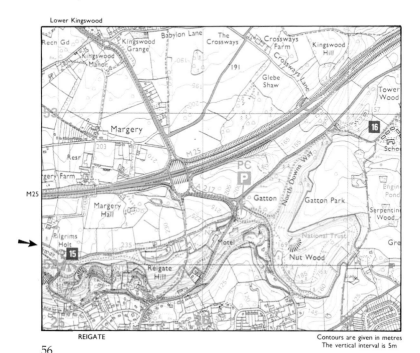

REIGATE

Contours are given in metres
The vertical interval is 5m

Church of St Andrew remains. It is lavishly decorated with treasures gathered by Lord Monson from all over Europe. A particular delight is the private family chapel, which has a fire-place, and is said to be one of the finest in the country. The keys to the chapel can be borrowed from Whitehall House, Rocky Lane, just outside North Lodge Gate.

Emerging from Gatton Park by a thatched gatehouse called North Lodge, you continue straight ahead on the road and then turn left. Where the driveway branches, take the right-hand fork and you find yourself on a gravel track. Keep left, entering Reigate Hill Golf Club at the kissing gate. The path is well marked through the club grounds, running parallel to the M25. A few years ago this land was all 'pick your own' fruit fields but it seems that the citizens of Surrey are now keener on picking the right club.

Aim towards a kissing gae that leads in to a narrow pathway between a meadow on the left and a cricket pitch on the right. Passing through another gate, you come to the gravel car park of Merstham Cricket Club. Continue along the partly metalled footpath and then out of the car park on to Quality Street which leads you to the village of Merstham on the out-skirts of Redhill.

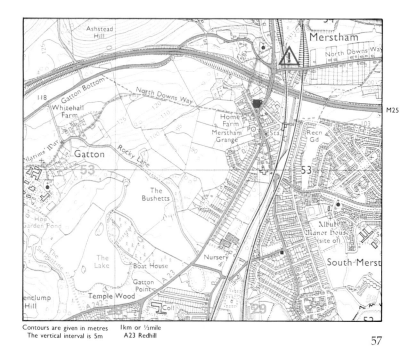

Contours are given in metres   1km or ½mile
The vertical interval is 5m   A23 Redhill

Box Hill

Box Hill, rising majestically to 563 feet (172 metres) from the valley of the River Mole at its foot, is owned by the National Trust, and the landscape, plants and animals are maintained and protected by the Trust through the Box Hill Management Committee. Because of its delightful woods, invigorating chalk upland air, and the fine views across the surrounding countryside, Box Hill has attracted visitors for many years. It was the coming of the railways, though, in 1849 that made it so popular with day trippers from London and other towns and cities of the busy south.

In 1971, Box Hill was declared an official Country Park with the aim of protecting its countryside while, at the same time, giving city dwellers the chance to breathe some fresh country air. Nowadays, as well as the work involved in maintaining the woodland, preventing the spread of scrub, and controlling soil erosion by rain, the Trust's workers must cope with the pressures of more than a million visitors every year.

The chalk that forms the bulk of Box Hill is capped with a deposit known as 'clay with flints'. This is probably derived from the chalk but, unlike that white rock, is much less permeable to the passage of water and therefore supports a different vegetation. On the plateau, as a consequence, there is mixed woodland with oak and birch, as well as the more acid-loving heathland plants. Although the chalk is porous, it tends to stay moist because, as the surface dries out, water tends to move upwards from the water table below by capillary action; this is why chalk grassland can remain surprisingly lush even in the driest of summers, if not too much water is extracted from the underlying aquifer, or deposit of rock containing water. Near Box Hill, indeed, there is evidence of a whole underground water system in the chalk.

As well as a rich natural history, which has brought Box Hill English Nature's designation of a Grade 1 Site of Special Scientific Interest (SSSI), there is much more of interest in the area. The North Downs Way crosses the A24 to the south of the Burford Bridge Hotel, which was once a small roadside inn that has played host to such distinguished visitors as Keats and Lord Nelson. Just to the north of the hotel is Flint Cottage, once the home of the poet and novelist George Meredith (1828–1909) who entertained, among others, Max Beerbohm and J. M. Barrie. Having crossed the Mole and climbed the steep river cliff, the Way passes just to the south of Swiss Cottage, where John Logie Baird (1888–1946), the Scottish inventor, is thought to have carried out some of his experiments with television. Nearby is the National Trust's information centre, shop and restaurant, and just to the north of that is the 19th century Box Hill Fort, built as a 'mobilisation centre' and redoubt, to play its part in repelling any likely invasion from the Continent. About 90 yards (82 metres) west of the fort is the so-called Peter Labellières Stone, which may mark the spot where this eccentric marine officer and local resident was buried upside-down, at his own request, after his death in 1880 – it is said that he made this strange request because '. . . as all the world is turned topsy-turvy . . .' he would be the right way up eventually.

The triangulation pillar on Box Hill is set at a height of 563 feet (172 metres) above sea level. There are fine views to be seen from here.

4 Merstham to Oxted

via Gravelly Hill
8 miles (12.9 km)

On reaching Quality Street in Merstham which, to the right, emerges by The Feathers public house, turn left opposite the White Cottage into an attractive residential road. Merstham quarries were famous for their sandstone in medieval times; although little-used locally, the stone was used to build Windsor Castle. Where the road comes to an end before a pillared driveway and just past a 'Tudor Building of Special Interest', The Old Forge **17**, turn right and cross the M25 on a footbridge. Continue along the metalled path, passing a pond on the left fringed with wild flowers. Soon you emerge on to a minor road where you turn right **A** opposite the attractive, flint-built church of St Katharine with its white clunch tower.

Cross the dual carriageway and carry on more or less straight across up Rockshaw Road. Cross the railway line on a brick bridge, and then cross another section of the line. Continue along the road for about half a mile (800 metres) and just before the house called 'Noddy's Hall' **B**, look out on the left-hand

With the decreasing use of herbicides and pesticides, arrays of glorious crimson poppies are gracing our fields in summer once more.

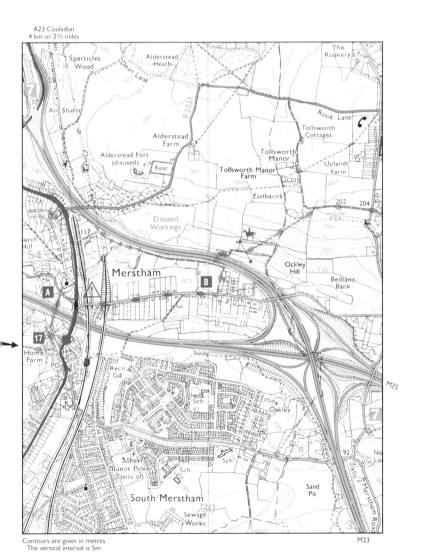

Contours are given in metres
The vertical interval is 5m

M23

side of the road for a finger-post pointing you to the left. You are now heading down towards the M23 through a grassy meadow with houses on your right. Go under the motorway and on to a gravel lane between banks thronging in early summer with wild flowers.

Where one track diverts to the left, go straight on and then diagonally up the hill. The track soon shrinks to a narrow bridleway and after a short distance you enter more arable fields and continue to climb. At the top of the hill, at a T-junction in the tracks, your way continues to the right. When you come to Hilltop Lane, go straight across on to a gravelled farm lane towards a rather grand-looking farmhouse, which you then pass on your left. Pass the house of 'Hilltop' with its clock on the front wall and take the right-hand lane where there are good views looking back towards Redhill. Where the lane forks again, with the middle fork going through some gates, your route is to the right. At a three-way post in Rook Lane, continue straight on. Keeping Willey Park farm on your right, walk on down the lane and do not turn right on the public bridleway. Where the lane forks, shortly after the farmhouse garden **C**, turn right.

Continue along the metalled, quiet country lane from which you eventually emerge on to the Stanstead Road between two brick pillars. Cross Stanstead Road and continue along War Coppice Road, passing a house called Arthur's Seat and the derelict folly of Whitehill Tower **18** on your left. Despite the trees, you get good views to both sides. You emerge from the trees by a house just before reaching Woodland Way. A glance at the map will reveal the locations of several of the fortified vantage points which have been erected on the downs at various times.

At the crossroads of Wealdway and Hextall's Lane cross the stile and follow the path, keeping War Coppice Road on your left. Rejoin the road by a grassy viewing area where you look

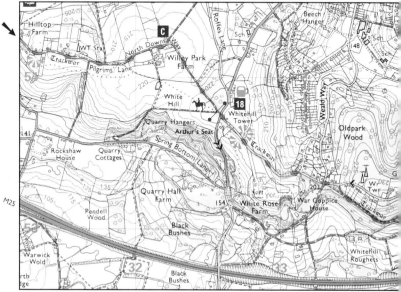

Contours are given in me
The vertical interval is .

across to the M25. Continue on up the road – this is Caterham viewpoint – and then turn right **D** just before the trees on to a surfaced track down through the woods.

At a sign indicating a permissive path to Winders Hill, turn right. The hill falls steeply away to the right and the path curves to the left down to a road. Turn right just before the road and cross the A22 on the footbridge **E**. Cross the stile into the field, cross another stile out of it and turn right up the lane and into the woods once more.

About 20 yards (18 metres) along the lane, look for a stile on the left-hand side taking you on to a track on the left, where you then reach a track heading downhill and some earth steps down on to a lane. Go straight across the lane and on to a woodland path once more, where some wooden steps emerge into a car parking area. Turn right on to a partly concreted lane, which leads towards Winders Hill Cottages, and pass a vineyard on your right. Follow the path, crossing a minor road at South Lodge and winding your way through Marden Park Wood. Marden Park is a Victorian gothic mansion, now a convent school. At Hanging Wood forest farm carry straight on and, just before reaching another minor road, turn left over a stile, and walk along the woodland-edge path that runs parallel to the road.

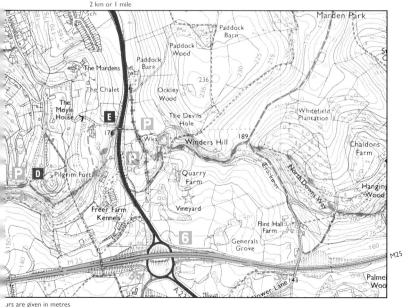

urs are given in metres
vertical interval is 5m

These timber-supported earth steps were built by conservation volunteers and lead the traveller steeply down the scarp slope of the North Downs.

After about 300 yards (275 metres), the track emerges on to the road again where you bear left on to the road.

At the next T-junction there is another minor road; turn right **F**, then bear right off the road on to a surfaced track that runs parallel to it for some distance. At the next finger-post, bear right a little, and then left through the trees above Oxted and the motorway. You can now make out the white chalk of the cement works as it carves into the hillside. At the next finger-post turn right down some steps and head straight towards the busy motorway and the railway line.

The Oxted Railway Tunnel **19** was built in 1878, and was a considerable engineering feat. But you should appreciate the more recent achievement of building this long, steep flight of timber-supported earth steps to bring the North Downs Way down a steep, south-facing chalk slope of Oxted Downs owned by the National Trust. Continue round to the left at the bottom of the steps, and you can now see Oxted clearly in the Weald below. Follow the narrow track through the woodland on the edge of the hanger. More than ten years on, the effects of the great storm of 1987 are still starkly evident in this beech wood. Self-seeded new growth is just starting to obstruct the views and decision will soon have to be made about which young trees should be culled. The Trail emerges onto open downland over-looking the motorway, and the limeworks is directly ahead. Soon after this, turn downhill to the right and into some fields, aiming towards the motorway and keeping the limeworks on your left, then turn left. When you reach the trees at the corner of the field, follow the line of the fence to a stile just by some houses, you soon emerge on to a road that leads down to Oxted. If you decide to walk into the town, where there are restaurants and accommodation, you will have about 2 miles (3.2 km) of suburban walking to cover.

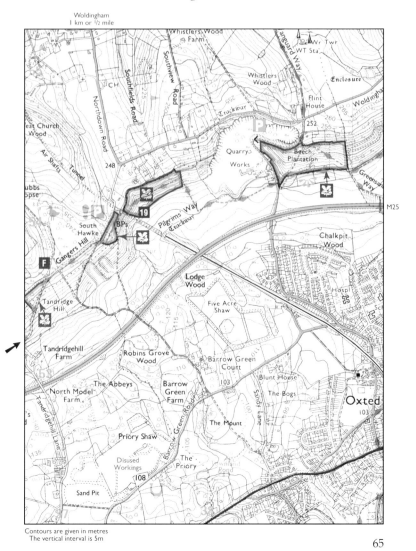

Contours are given in metres
The vertical interval is 5m

Use and conservation of the North Downs escarpment

A glance at the map quickly shows that Surrey is a land-locked county, and many conservationists and naturalists who live in the area seem to regard the scarp with much the same fascination that coastal dwellers have for a shoreline and for which it offers them a kind of substitute; indeed, the scarp has in the past been just that. Some believe, however, that it is only in the last couple of decades that they have begun to learn how to look after it.

In the past, as earlier maps clearly demonstrate, surprisingly large areas of even the steeper slopes have been cultivated, and, dating from further back in time still, the parish boundaries run in elongated rectangles from the lower flat lands of the Weald, or at least those areas underlain by the Greensand to the south, up to the crest of the Downs themselves. Then, to the north, these rectangles run down the dip slope towards the region where the London Clay determines the geology and geography. While this portrait of the area may be a generally accurate one, many variations do occur, in the same way that the natural history shows local differences. The question arises, 'What was the purpose of such a parcelling up of the land?'

Again, conservationists in the area suggest that dividing the land in this way enabled each parish to enjoy a share of each of the main soil types, so that there was adequate grazing land for sheep, cattle or pigs, areas where timber and bracken could be cropped for fuel, building purposes and animal bedding, and areas that could be set aside for arable crops. And, even at a local level, the ridge of the Downs would have provided a common droveway between the parishes. Consequently (and this is very noticeable), apart from the ridge route, the majority of the traditional footpaths and rights of way run in a north–south direction, while the current system of east–west communications seems to be of comparatively modern origin.

Clearly, in its length between just north of Guildford to about Sevenoaks in Kent, the M25 is just such a modern east–west route. Some local planners believe that the way the motorway has been brought up the North Downs near Reigate, for example, was well thought-out although, further eastwards, walkers along the escarpment may find the noise from it intrusive at first as the sound travels upwards. As well as traffic noise, there is the near-continual sound of commercial and military aircraft, with Gatwick and Heathrow airports only a stone's throw away and the army's use of the North Downs as a navigational aid for the helicopters on their way to continental Europe.

Among the more recent threats to the integrity of the North Downs' natural history is drilling for oil. In Surrey alone there have been some 20 exploratory wells, but only three of them have shown signs of commercial viability and, in any case, apart from one to the south of Box Hill, they are largely concealed by woodland. There has, of course, been a long tradition of quarrying the chalk from the Downs, as the number of disused pits clearly demonstrates, and sands from the Greensand have also been extracted. In the past, far less regard was given to conservation aspects of exploitation than it is today and, although the work continues, it is now subject to some degree of planning control.

The United Kingdom is thought to contain half the world's remaining chalk grassland, and perhaps 10 per cent of this is in Kent and Surrey. Since the Second World War there significant decline in both the extent and the quality of this habitat; much has been lost to invading scrub or destroyed by modern farming methods.

Since grazing ceased on some parts of the ridge, and with the temporary disappearance of the rabbit population (now quickly recovering, of course) due to myxomatosis, bracken scrub has thrived in some areas. Local volunteer groups have been very active, however, in cutting back the scrub and, when this has been achieved, the downland grass can more easily be maintained by such techniques as carefully controlled winter grazing by sheep. Much of the North Downs ridge in Surrey is managed by the National Trust, and other parts by local authorities, which have made considerable efforts to maintain the North Downs' essential grassland character. Today, nearly 90 per cent of the surviving unimproved chalk grassland is designated as protected, but there is much for future generations to do if this unique landscape is to be preserved.

White scars of chalk gleaming through the vegetation show how extensively

lime-rich rock has been quarried from the downs in the past.

5 Oxted to Otford

past Knockholt Pound
$11\frac{3}{4}$ miles (18.9 km)

On this stretch of the walk you will cross the border from Surrey into Kent. Somehow, after a refreshing night's stop, the climb through a suburban setting back up to the North Downs Way seems less daunting than the descent. The finger-post on the road leading down to Oxted indicates that you turn right here, although this is not obvious from the map. Walk about 50 yards (45 metres) down the road and, on the left-hand side, look for a concealed flight of steps **A** up into the hedgerow. Walk up the shrubbery tunnel to the stile and then fork left uphill. You come to another stile which leads into Oxted Down National Trust land; you turn right at the fork, so that you are walking parallel to the motorway with a wire fence on the right and hawthorn on the left.

Here the National Trail leads you by Titsey Plantation on the Oxted Downs, where walkers can follow the Titsey Foundation Walk.

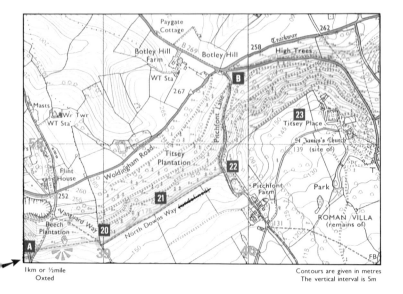

1km or ½mile
Oxted

Contours are given in metres
The vertical interval is 5m

At the next stile, turn right downhill towards the motorway on a tree-lined track, which is also the Vanguard Way **20** and a link route to the Greensand Way on the other side of the motorway. Bear left with the track and go over another stile. You are now on the Titsey Estate **21** where your route continues straight on along the line of the Downs.

Climb a stile and follow the path, keeping the woodland on your left. At the top corner of the field cross another stile, walk down some steps, and turn left up a sunken lane. Soon, on the left-hand side, a gate leads to a viewpoint overlooking a house and grounds. I have sat and enjoyed this view for hours on end and highly recommend the short detour if you have time to spare. The lane you are now following is Pitchfork Lane **22**, which rises to Botley Hill and seems to take you back half a century in time.

Turn right on to the B269, signposted to Limpsfield, Edenbridge and Oxted and, across the road, look for a finger-post that points you towards an acorn marker **B** in the trees. Continue along the woodland path running parallel to the road; but by a large beech tree turn left up some steps – there is a rustic wooden railing to help you. Go over two stiles, bearing a little to the right, and you can look over Titsey Place **23**. Descend some steps, turn right along a minor road and then immediately left into the woods again. After another double stile crossing you will emerge into some rough arable fields,

71

where you continue straight ahead and then left a little towards some more trees. Go over a stile concealed in the hedge and follow the path along the top of the field keeping the wood to your left. Walk past the field gate close to the road **C** but continue to skirt the northern edge of the field, crossing another stile and after 50 yards (45 metres) turn right **D** into the woods to join the road (B2024). Cross the road and walk to the right along Chestnut Avenue passing Park Wood Golf Club. You will come to a T-junction in the lane by a postbox, where you turn right, continuing on through an expensive-looking residential area. Eventually the metalled lane becomes a gravelled track and begins to descend. The Kent/Surrey border is marked by a milestone.

You emerge from the lane and come to a road where a green public footpath sign **E** on the opposite side of the road points your way. Go through a low hedge, over a stile and round to the left on the edge of a field. Simply follow the path as it curves to the right. The route twists and turns through the woods, so follow the waymarks with care.

At **F** the yellow arrow points up the hill, keeping a line of trees to the left. Another stile soon comes into view; cross it and follow the track, emerging on to a rough lane. The North Downs Way takes you to the right and along the top edge of a field with, below you, the buildings that make up Pilgrim House **24**. You soon come to another rustic stile, where you carry on along the path, following the track along the left-hand side of the meadow with the line of trees to your left.

At the corner of the field, follow the path round to the right and walk on towards a double stile in the corner of the field

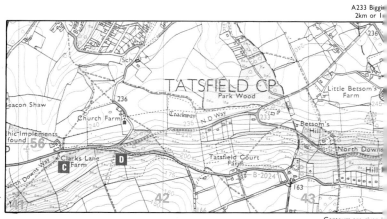

Contours are given i
The vertical interva

where you continue straight on. Carry on round the left-hand corner of the field and, about halfway up the field, turn left and look for a concealed stile on your left, then turn right. The narrow path takes you past a house with swimming pool and tennis court.

As the path turns right, fork left, crossing a stile. Follow the path through pleasant old beech woodland, but just before reaching a stile, turn right down the left-hand edge of a field. Walk along the line of a wire fence and in the corner of the field turn left across a stile into the next field. Keep to the right-hand edge this time, with a minor road on your right **G**, eventually you come to a stile at the far end which leads out onto a minor road.

Cross the road and enter the next field by another stile, then follow the left-hand edge of the field. Climb over another pair of stiles, cross the road and go into the next field. Pass through a hedge by way of another stile and continue round the left-hand edge of the field, with the road just the other side of the high hedge **H**.

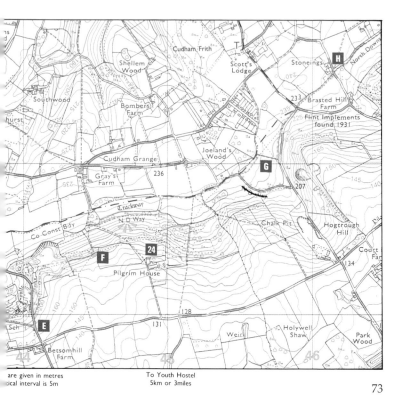

are given in metres
tical interval is 5m

To Youth Hostel
5km or 3miles

A mile (1.6 km) or so to the south of Knockholt Pound is Chevening House, probably designed by Inigo Jones in the seventeenth century.

Over another stile in the corner of the field, keep going along the left-hand edge of the meadow, where you cross a stile in the corner of the field and then another double stile almost immediately afterwards. After this, turn right into the next field with two radio masts on the skyline in front of you.

Continue on the same line into the next field. At the next field boundary there is an acorn on the post indicating that you should turn to the left along the broad, grassy track. At the top of the field, skirt the hedge, turning right along the main grassy track. The track now bears to the right and emerges next to a narrow road, where you turn left, for 50 yards (45 metres) before exiting the field at some steps. You then cross the road and, having climbed the stile, follow the right-hand edge of the field.

Turn right onto the edge of some woodland. Keep the woodland on your right-hand side and as you head eastwards you will see the houses of Knockholt Pound **25** below. On a clear

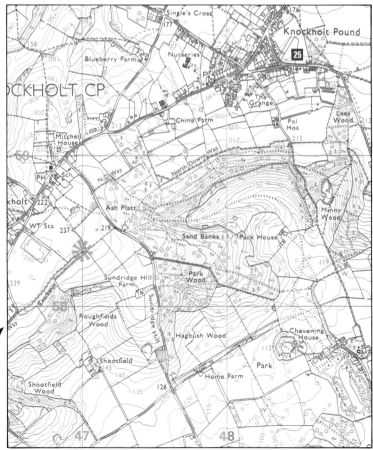

Contours are given in metres
The vertical interval is 5m

day, you will catch a sight of London beyond the houses – the
Canary Wharf Tower, its laser beacon flashing. It seems
strange to get this sudden glimpse of London, apparently so
close at hand. But, in fact, the National Trail actually skirts the
Greater London boundary for a mile or two and it is perfectly
possible to be back in the centre of the city wihin half an hour
from here by train. In fact, at this point, it is only the narrow
band of the downland and its scarp that separates the two
probing fingers of commuterland – Orpington to the north and
Sevenoaks to the south.

Cross a stile located near a brick bungalow and turn right
on to the road then, almost immediately, turn left. The North
Downs Way is now straight ahead.

On reaching the woods, the path bears to the right following the woodland edge around the field. Cross the stile to the right and turn left to emerge back into the field, crossing another stile which leads you out onto the ridge of the downs. Turn left, walking round the edge of the field with woods on your left. Down to the right lies the red-brick Chevening House, the official country residence of the British Foreign Secretary. The great mansion was built between 1616 and 1630 to a design by Inigo Jones and acquired by James Stanhope, later Lord Stanhope, in 1718. Successive generations of the Stanhope family altered and extended the house considerably before presenting it to the nation in 1959. It was their wish that it should be used by the Prime Minister, a cabinet minister or a member of the royal family. In fact, since the 7th Earl of Stanhope died in 1967, it has served as home to, among others, Edward Heath, Lord Hailsham and Prince Charles.

Descend round the left-hand edge of the field, keeping the woods on your left. Following the contours of the hill now, you soon come to another stile and take the well-defined path across the meadow, keeping a couple of trees to your right. Walk into the trees again and cross yet another stile, following the footpath as it contours the hill. You then start to descend towards the busy roads. In the bottom corner of the field, cross a stile in the

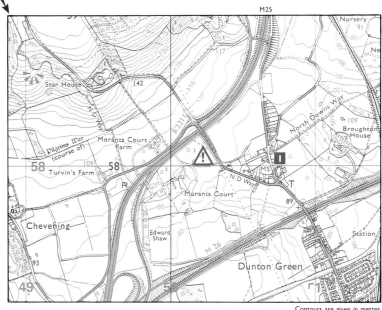

Contours are given in metres
The vertical interval is 5m

hedgerow and then follow the line of the field round to the left and then right, heading down towards a stile and the road beyond.

Turn right on to the Sevenoaks Road, and go across the M25. Where the Sevenoaks road bears round to the right, turn left by the Rose and Crown, signposted to Otford and Shoreham. Just before you get to the Donnington Manor Hotel and Restaurant, turn right **I** on to a footpath.

Go over a stile and on to a field-edge path, then over another stile, and carry on up the hill. Where the track appears to fork in front of a large sycamore tree, bear right into the woodlands on a well-defined but narrow path. At the junction, cross the broad track and continue on across the large field.

Having crossed the field you will come to a stile leading on to a railway bridge, which you cross before joining the descent to Otford on the metalled road (Telston Lane). Follow the drive downwards, turning left in front of Oast Cottage. When you emerge from the drive onto the road, go straight on, passing a newsagent on your left. When you arrive at the main road, you turn right.

You have now arrived in the smart high street of Otford **26**, with its grand houses and fine lawns, as well as shops and several pubs.

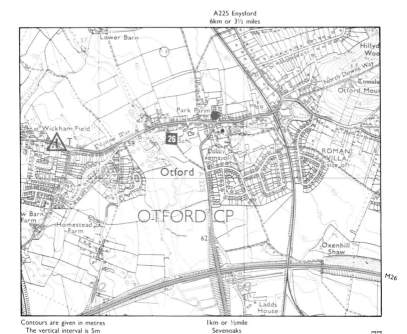

A225 Enysford
6km or 3½ miles

1km or ½mile
Sevenoaks

Contours are given in metres
The vertical interval is 5m

Some aspects of the natural history of the Surrey Hills

The animals and plants of the North Downs in Surrey enjoy an advantage that their southerly counterparts across the Weald do not – the North Downs scarp slope faces southwards, so that it benefits from the sun and is sheltered from the colder weather of the north. Similarly, the ridge forms a natural stopping-off point for any birds or insects passing across southern England. There is also great variety in the available habitats. It has been said that it is possible to see as many species in an hour of searching on a given area of the North Downs as you could see in a year in a similar area of Scotland – the species would be different, of course! For example, there are perhaps 300 different kinds of plants to be seen and, in some areas, as many as 40 species of butterflies have been observed in a single year. In just one morning in May, a local naturalist identified 15 different species of butterflies.

Another significant feature of the wildlife of the North Downs is the variation from one chalk hill to another. While there are many plants and animals that are common to the whole region, it is rare for any two areas to have identical species' lists. For example, even those plants such as drop-wort, mallow and valerian, which are found growing in many

One of the floral delights of the North Downs Way is viper's bugloss with its funnel-shaped, blue flowers appearing in June and July.

parts of the North Downs, do so irregularly. Doubtless this results from differences in local geological and climatic conditions.

A good general introduction to the natural history of the chalk hills of Surrey may be gained by following the National Trust's recommended nature walk on their property at Box Hill, for which they provide an explanatory map and leaflet for a very modest price. Typical of chalk hills, the beech is a common tree here, although there are also wild cherry, larch and pine, box, yew, and juniper, as well as ash and silver birch, willow and elder, hazel and horse chestnut. And, among the shrubs, there is blackthorn and hawthorn, dogwood and spindle trees, wayfaring trees and privet. Such a variety of trees is reflected in the bird and mammal life, and you may well be lucky enough to catch sight of a shy roe deer or a bulky badger. Of rabbits there are plenty and, as a consequence, their main predator, the red fox, is also abundant. Another aspect of the chalk ridge is that it provides warm updraughts of air on which rooks can frolic and tumble or kestrels soar in search of insects and small mammals – indeed, on one occasion, I saw five of these 'windhovers' at the same time.

The fruits and berries of a number of British plants are known to be poisonous, but walkers along the North Downs Way should be wary of two particular wildlife hazards: adders and the seemingly innocent plant, wild parsnip, with its yellow umbelliferous flower heads, which blossom between June and September. A hot summer brings large numbers of adders out to bask on the dry chalk hillsides. Usually, if disturbed, an adder will slither quietly away and, for the most part, its jaws are too small to be any threat to an adult. But a barefoot child, a family dog, or anyone poking an investigating hand into a bankside hole might surprise Britain's only venomous reptile and be bitten. Even then, the bite is not usually fatal to a healthy adult but, at the very least, it could be painful and put an end to your walk.

Wild parsnip is related to, and resembles, well-known hedgerow plants such as cow parsley, but it is the only member of the family to produce yellow flowers during mid- to late summer in the area. Only a small number of people are vulnerable to its effects but, if a susceptible person handles the plant or touches it accidentally, it removes some protection against ultraviolet light from the skin, causing a sunburn-like effect. In a few cases, sufferers have needed hospital treatment.

6 Otford to Medway Bridge

through Wrotham
17¼ miles (27.8 km)

Continue through the village of Otford **26** and, when you get to the mini-roundabout, take the first exit on your left up the hill towards Otford Station. At the first crossroads past the station, turn right. Walk along Pilgrims' Way East and, after about 50 yards (45 metres), look out for the marker post on the left-hand side of the road, pointing left off the road up a narrow path. It is a steepish climb to start the day but, as you rise higher, there are some steps in the track and then, with a memorial seat in sight, the path becomes a broad, grassy track. There are fine views from here back across the Darent valley, only slightly marred by the motorway which cuts across the landscape. Gradually the route seems to level out and, towards the top of the hill, you arrive at a grassy meadow. Take the right-hand path across the field and pass by the triangulation pillar on your left, cross the stile and emerge on to the road **A**, continuing effec-

Coldrum Stones Long Barrow is the remains of one of a number of neolithic burial chambers used for interment.

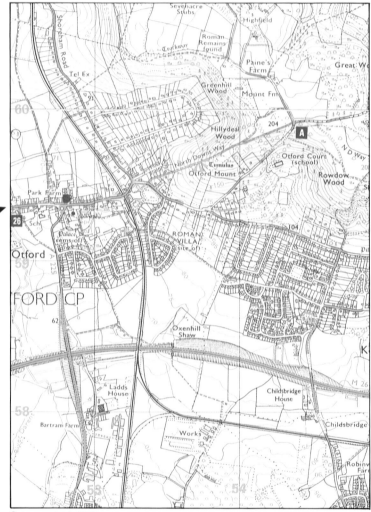

Contours are given in metres
The vertical interval is 5m

tively straight ahead, and following the signpost towards Woodland Easthill and West Kingsdown.

After walking about 100 yards (90 metres) along the road, pass through the gate on the right and skirt a field. Cross another field before reaching a farmhouse, pass through four more kissing gates before reaching the minor road in front of Silverdale Cottage. Turn right here and walk up the road, turning left at the gate towards Otford Manor along a private drive.

At the end of the line of white posts, before entering the manor grounds, cross over a stile **B** on the right and turn on to a narrow path, with woodland to your right and a fence to your left. Follow the path as it bears round the left of the field and dives downhill into a nature reserve run by the Kent Trust for Nature Conservation. The path follows the contours eastwards, above Kemsing. The youth hostel, which was once the vicarage attached to the Norman church of St Mary the Virgin, is situated one-third of a mile (500 metres) away. Follow the waymarks as you pass over stiles and through woodland. On the crest of a hill is a wooden cross on a brick pillar. As you reach the end of the open downland, turn left, cross another stile and enter the meadow. Kemsing is well worth a visit, it is famous for the healing spring of St Edith's Well, said to cure sore eyes. Named after King Edgar's daughter, who was born in Kemsing in 961, the well drew many visitors and, although the stone-ringed well-head is now covered in, it still attracts them.

Your route goes round to the right. In the corner of the field, cross two more stiles on to a path, ignoring the other forks. Go over a further stile and into a meadow which contains jumps for horses, here your way continues along the right-hand edge of the field.

After crossing two more stiles and about 100 yards (90 metres) before you reach the boundary of a house, turn right into the wood again over a stile, and through a gate before turning left on to a path. Cross another stile on to

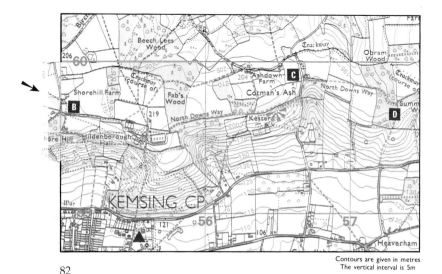

Contours are given in metres
The vertical interval is 5m

a minor road, where you turn left uphill. You have just emerged from the grounds known as Kester. Pass Cotman's Ash Farm and look out on the right by some farm buildings at Highfields farm for the North Downs Way acorn mark and post **C**. Cross the stile and follow the path between a farm lane to your left and a house drive to your right, then cross another stile and follow a line of posts across the meadow. After the next stile, follow the left-hand edge of the field, then go left over a stile back on to a woodland path.

You emerge from the woods into arable fields, continue straight on along a gravel track at **D**, following a line of trees. Then, at a junction of lanes **E**, continue straight ahead. Follow the line of the hills and the broad farm track.

When you reach some trees, look out for an acorn marker in the trees by a stile taking you a little to the left and into the woodland, passing an old flint-built dew pond. You skirt the right-hand edge of a big field, go through a little gate and into the woods, and you soon arrive down a tree archway on to a road, where there is an obvious marker post pointing right **F**. Turn right along the road and then immediately left and walk down the steps in the woods to admire the view at the field boundary. Cross a stile, and aim downhill to the next stile. Cross it and follow the obvious path across the arable field towards the road. Just before reaching the road, turn left **G** on to the stony farm track.

After about half a mile (800 metres) of fairly steady walking along the farm track you come to a road again, which you cross right and then left, and enter another track by a gate. You are now on a narrow path beneath the hills and hedges obscure

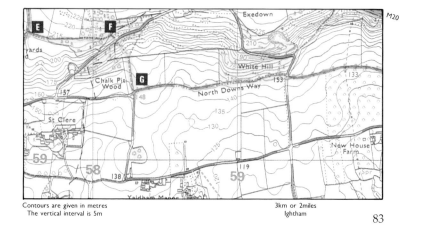

Contours are given in metres
The vertical interval is 5m

3km or 2miles
Ightham

83

the views, but you soon arrive at the houses of Wrotham **27**, pronounced 'Rootham'. When you arrive at the tarmac road, continue straight on and at the Give Way sign continue straight across the road and into Pilgrims' Way again. Just past the tennis court turn left up the tarmac bridleway to continue on the national trail. Cross the busy main road and turn left towards the roundabout – you are now going over the M20. At the roundabout, take the first minor road to the right into Pilgrims' Way. After 100 yards (90 metres) leave the road and follow a parallel path, which rejoins the road at the house called 'Chaucers' **28**. The path meanders between the road and fields all along this stretch. Walk along the road and at a stile on the left that bears the legend 'farmland, private, please keep to footpath', cross and walk along the edge of the field by the road.

The path rejoins the road and you continue on up it until the Way takes you back into the field again and up the right-hand edge. At the top right-hand corner of the field cross a stile into a wood. The path eventually comes to a track – turn left and, just before reaching a gate, the track splits **H** and your way forks to the left, going uphill through the woodland, and you are rising on to the chalk downs once more. This is Trottiscliffe Down **29**.

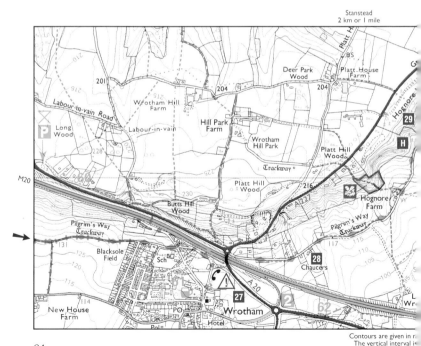

Contours are given in r
The vertical interval is

Where the path levels out, you come to a high brick wall, in whose shadow you walk. Pass by a red-brick lodge and continue on up the track until you arrive at the road, where you turn right towards the crossroads.

Turn right at the Vigo Inn, keeping the pub on your left. A landlord of earlier times was a naval veteran who purchased the inn with prize money won in a battle against French and Spanish ships in 1702. Just before you reach a flint-built bridge **30** across the road, turn left up the steps, and cross a bridleway into Trosley Country Park. Keep to the right, following the main track with the visitor centre on your left.

Continue straight on, following the main track. Where there is a gas marker you start to climb the hill, bearing left. Go through the gate at the top of the rise, turn right **I** down the hill. At the bottom by some houses the North Downs Way turns left.

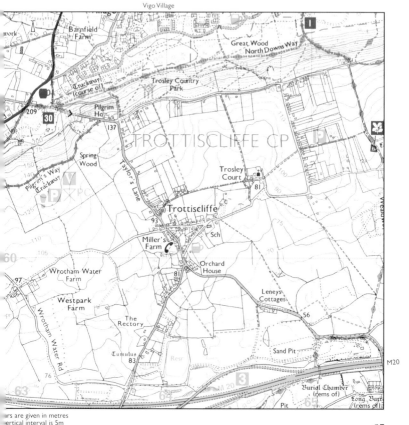

The flinty way you have been walking along for some time seems to have been constructed for the ease of foot travellers, and makes you think that perhaps the car is not here for ever, after all.

You are now walking along the near-bottom edge of the escarpment again. This is good long-distance path walking: quiet, peaceful, with only the slight roar of the motorway to the right, few people, plenty of plants and good views. Downs rise up to your left.

Where a track comes in from the right and there is a square brick building, continue straight on without gaining height for another 100 yards (90 metres) until you reach a crossroads in an opening.

Turn left and cross a stile, walk along a fence-lined track up the hill towards the escarpment and trees. Pass a stile and follow to the right. You are now rising diagonally up the scarp on a grassy track, crossing a further short stile with hawthorn and dog rose on either side. This is good chalk grassland, much of which is managed in a fashion that assists in its preservation. Turn left and before a steep, mercifully short, climb you arrive at the road just to the right of three beech trees. This is Holly Hill **31**.Looking down at the broad valley below, you can see the channel out by the River Medway as it flows across the distant Weald, through Maidstone and down towards its broad estuary. The big house in the foreground is Birling Place. Landowners in this area are facing increasing pressures due to the expansion of the Medway towns, with fires, vandalism and the dumping of household rubbish causing much damage to the amenities of the district.

Continue straight over at the road onto Holly Hill, passing the lodge, then at The Bungalow, where again the 'No Through Road' signs appear and where there is a car park on the left, look on the right, and, hidden by the roadside, is a concrete marker telling you to go straight on. Continue past the drive way to Holly Hill House and, eventually, by the house's west wing, the road becomes a track. Shortly afterwards, take the right fork of the track on the better-surfaced of the two lanes.

Continue through Matthewdown Wood and then Greatpark Wood, in a north-north-easterly direction, until you arrive at a crossing of the ways before reaching a line of pylons. Turn diagonally right here and pass beneath two rows of pylons, where you then cross a lane **J**. Continue, crossing a stile to the left and heading across an arable field.

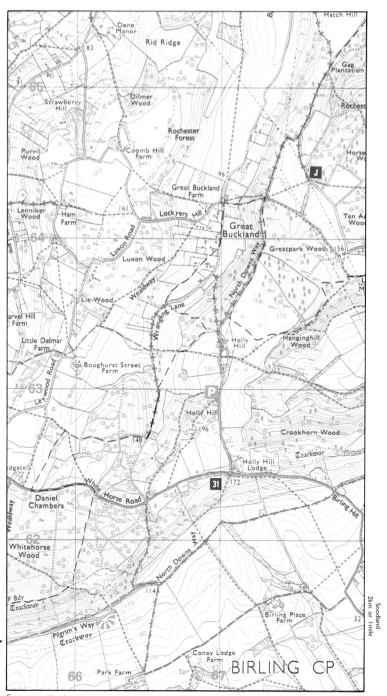

Contours are given in metres
The vertical interval is 5m

Towards the Medway valley and Snodland. It is not obvious here, but Snodl

has been called 'Kent's Middlesbrough'.

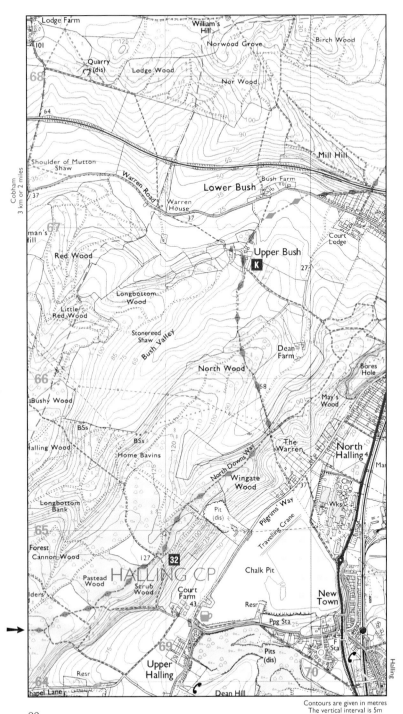

Contours are given in metres
The vertical interval is 5m

90

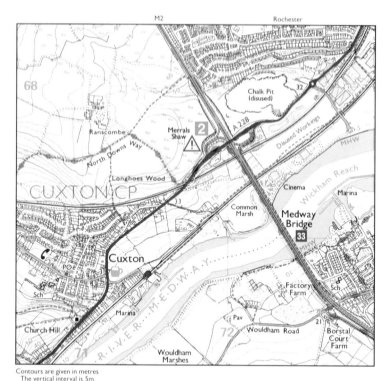

Contours are given in metres
The vertical interval is 5m

The track is well surfaced and there is a kissing gate in a patchwork of woodland and fields.

At a five-way junction of paths **32** take the second right, keeping left at the fork 20 yards on through managed beech woodland. Cross under a further set of pylons, descending to fork left at another pylon dropping steeply into a field. Cross the valley track leading up the other side into North Wood. At the end of the woods cross a stile into a field to a spur trees. The path passes the attractive buildings at Upper Bush, soon becoming a track **K** and then a road. Turn right down the hill, at the bend in the road head across the fields to the right, turning right at the road and then immediately left up to the railway behind the houses. At the bridge turn left and cross the bridge, then go right, down some steps into a field.

Continue on past the next right-hand turn to the south of Ranscombe and then take the next right on the road. This leads down the hill towards the railway again, where you turn left and follow the road. Before you reach the M2 motorway, turn right to pass over the railway and arrive down at the road near the Medway Bridge **33**.

The Medway Bridge, carrying the M2 as well as the national trail footway,

Dickens's Rochester

The route of the North Downs Way actually crosses the river on a footpath carried by the Medway Bridge, and it therefore misses out the centre of Rochester, but a short diversion into the town is well worth the effort. If you should find yourself spending the night at the 400-year-old coaching inn, The Royal Victoria and Bull Hotel in the High Street, then you will be staying at the place which Charles Dickens called 'The Bull' in *Pickwick Papers* and 'The Blue Boar' in *Great Expectations*. Its present name was assumed following an overnight stop at the inn by Princess, soon to be Queen, Victoria.

Situated by a Z-shaped bend of the River Medway, Rochester and Chatham have played an important part in British history at least since Roman times. The neighbouring towns of Rochester and Chatham have much to offer today's visitors, including the magnificent cathedral (the second oldest in England), one of the best-preserved Norman castles to be seen anywhere, and the historic dockyard of Chatham which, for 400 years, was the main ship-building and repair dock for the Royal Navy, until it closed finally in 1988. But even the most casual of visitors to Rochester cannot fail to notice the many allusions to the journalist and novelist, Charles Dickens.

marks a change of scenery.

The son of an official in the Royal Navy Pay Office, Dickens was born in Portsmouth in the same momentous year, 1812, that saw Napoleon's retreat from Moscow and the destruction of his Grand Army. Less than five years later, the family moved to Chatham to a house that is now occupied by Chatham Railway Station. Dickens's most impressionable early years were spent within sight and sound of the inns, the castle, the cathedral and all the many trades associated with building Britain's fighting ships of the day. He often walked with his father around the area and, in 1856, was able to buy the house of Gads Hill Place in Higham, a couple of miles to the north, a house that he had admired as a child when on his walks. He took up walking again in later years and, because he had described the seven miles between Rochester and Maidstone as '. . . one of the most beautiful walks in England', it seems reasonable to assume that he was describing that same countryside that travellers on the North Downs Way still admire today.

Dickens died in 1870 and, although he had expressed a wish to be buried in the moat of his beloved Rochester Castle, this was not possible. His importance as a novelist was recognised, however, through his interment at Westminster Abbey.

7 Medway Bridge to Hollingbourne

via Detling
15¼ miles (24.5 km)

The easiest way to get back to the Medway Bridge, if you have spent the night in Rochester, is by taxi. It is a short journey by car and not expensive. Leave Rochester on the busy A228 (page 91) and turn left at the junction with the M2. A marker post points to the North Downs Way, leading on to the footbridge section of the Medway Bridge **33**. To your left are the heights of Rochester Castle and the spire of the cathedral, with the power station chimney immediately behind. After you have begun your crossing of the Medway Bridge, which carries the busy and noisy M2 motorway, it seems to take a long time before you ever reach the river itself. On the other hand, the waters themselves are soon crossed. On the other side of the bridge, there is a sign on the M2 which tells you that here you are only 45 miles (72 km) by road from Dover. On foot, via the Trail, it is a little further – 53 miles (88 km), or 59 miles (98 km) via Canterbury – but there is no doubt which is the pleasanter way to travel!

Once across the bridge, the footpath descends towards the M2. At the minor road, turn right and immediately left **A** into Nashenden Farm Lane. Where the lane forks to the right near some telegraph poles by a cluster of houses and grain stores, go right down the slope, and then keep left up the hill with a row of cottages on your left, and a white-painted building on your right. You now have the first ascent since crossing the river. Where two lines of trees meet in the corner, the marker post takes you on uphill, keeping the taller trees on your left.

Carry straight on up the hill along the narrow path and, where the path emerges on to a stony lane, fork left up the lane; do not turn immediately left into the field. The stony way continues to ascend slowly and, when you emerge from the trees, you can see that you have left Rochester some distance behind. You are now walking along Hill Road, crossing Wouldham Common, and it could be muddy in wet weather. Continue on past the driveway to Keeper's Lodge, and pass a couple of corrugated barns with the old wooden barn behind.

There is a footpath off to the right, but your way continues straight on to the metalled road, passing a white bungalow.

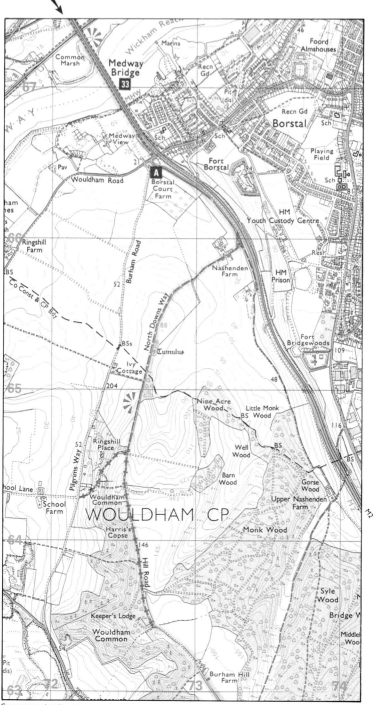

Contours are given in metres
The vertical interval is 5m

95

Pass by the drive to the lonely but popular Robin Hood pub and continue straight on along the road, passing a neatly trimmed hedge, fronted by tree stumps. You are now on Common Road, and you pass the iron gates of Fair View, aptly named as it looks east across the Weald, turn right at the signposted gap in the hedge, forking left over a stile into Blue-bell Hill picnic site **34**. The path dives a little down the hill then contours the down. Pass the car park, continuing onto a stile. Cross the stile and turn right onto a metalled bridleway which runs parallel to the busy A229.

You are now descending on a metalled bridleway and should ignore any paths to the right. Ignore the stiled footpath also off to the right, and continue journeying along the metalled path around the edge of the hill. The path emerges on to a road where you continue straight on, passing by the villa-style White Lodge down on the hillside to your right. The road soon arrives at the dual carriageway, but the track continues parallel with the A229 and you walk alongside the busy road. You may be tempted to cross the A229 via the footbridge but, instead, just continue down the road. Opposite a one-way road by an 'Old Chatham Road' sign, look out for a set of stone steps on the right indicating the North Downs Way. Descend the steps on to a sunken, wooden track then look out on the right of the track for an entrance into the field where Kit's Coty House Burial Chamber **35** is guarded by iron railings. There are now just three huge stones with a cap stone. These stones were in the burial chamber in the eastern end of a Neolithic long barrow, dating from about 2000 BC. They were originally covered by an earth mound some 180 feet (55 metres) long. This site is now managed by English Heritage. The stones themselves look as if they might be Green-sand, although the fact that they are pock-marked with what appear to be solution holes suggests that the stone has a lime content, too. With the stones standing at least 10 feet (3 metres) high, Kit's Coty House is an impressive place. Graffiti is not new, and some of the carvings date back to 1875.

Carry on down the lane to the road. This is a crossing of three roads; you turn immediately left **B** and then cross the road on to Pilgrims' Way. Little Kit's Coty House is further down the road to the right. This area is so rich in archaeological remains that it is often referred to as 'the Kentish Stonehenge'. All the sites, like the Coldrum Stones near Trosley, date from the Neolithic period and are, without exception, burial places. Continue on along the narrow tree-lined track, rising up on to a narrow road with pylons to your right, then turn left and almost immediately right to pass beneath the A229 Maidstone road through an unusually shaped underpass. You arrive by the forecourt of a garage and car sales, where a sign tells you to fork left on to the lane past Warren Cottage. Refreshments can be had here and a short walk along the A229 sliproad will bring you to Sand Barn, a museum run by Kent Wildlife Trust.

The lane soon becomes a chalky track and gradually ascends. Some steps on your right lead you to the solitary White Horse Stone **36**, a standing stone with two or three smaller stones in front of it. A few yards further on the way forks and the marker post indicates that your route is to the left off the main track.

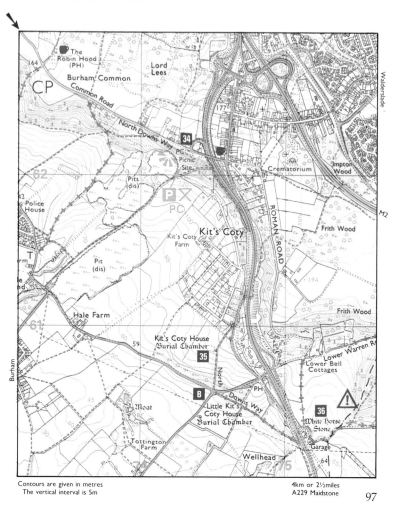

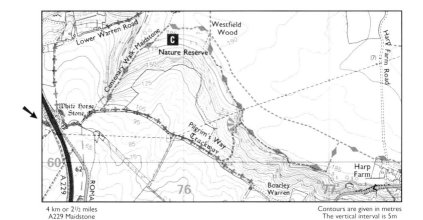

Contours are given in metres
The vertical interval is 5m

Turn right at the fork in the path. The steep ascent to a height of some 600 feet (185 metres) is reminiscent of the Box Hill climb. Pass another mile post and where the going begins to level out, the track bears to the right and passes a great oak with its partly hollowed trunk. Where the woods come to an end, standing stones have been made use of. Turn right here **C** and walk along the edge of a large field, keeping the woodland to your right.

When you get to the corner of the wood, follow the waymark. Continue round the edge of the field, following the line of the wood, and pass beneath the electricity cables. Just beyond, look for the gap in the hedge taking you down into the trees to the right and, after a few yards, turn left. It is a narrow, bramble-lined path through the woods along the edge of the ridge.

When you reach a marker post, turn left and go slightly uphill out of the woods again along a broad farm track with new trees. There is a farmhouse and farm buildings to your right, and the track soon bears to the right towards them. At Harp Farm turn right on to the road. Where Harp Farm Road emerges on to a more major road, go straight ahead and into the woods.

The church **37** is worth a visit down at Boxley. As you enter the woods go straight on. Continue on this bridleway, following the track, with the woods to your south. Eventually the track begins to descend and becomes narrower.

At the narrow sunken lane, turn right **D** into the lane but, after just a few yards, turn left across a stile, rather than continue on down it. Follow the waymarking carefully here; this may change in the future if a better crossing of the A249 can be negotiated at the bottom of Detling Hill. The new high-speed rail link to the Channel Tunnel is to go under the road here and there is a local campaign to improve the whole junction at Detling, which is at present an accident black spot. The new Trail crossing is likely to follow the sunken track to the junction of the Pilgrim's Way and Harple Lane.

Aim diagonally across the field to the gate and fence opposite. Go straight across the next field towards the stile and a gap in the fence, from where you head slightly right towards an obvious stile and begin the steep descent to Detling. At the busy dual carriageway, you turn left **E** and walk up the hill on a path beside the road. Pass the layby and walk until you reach a signpost beside the path. Turn right and cross the A249.

Pass through the metal barrier and walk down a flight of concrete steps. The path continues down through dense scrub before you enter an open field with a panoramic view over the Weald. Turn left along the edge of the trees and continue to walk along the eroded chalk hillside. A house appears before you, turn right here and cross the corner of the field to the woodland on the right of the house.

As you climb slightly, pass the wood on your left. Walk to the corner of it and continue straight ahead, along the boundary of the arable field. Before you a valley cuts into the scarp and to your left a small wood clings to the steep side of the

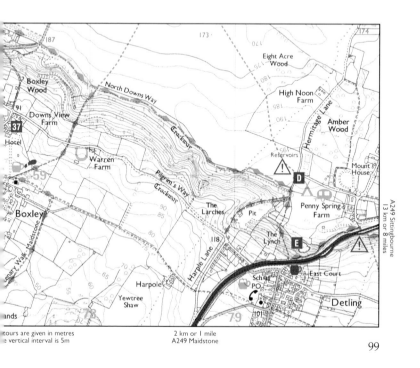

tours are given in metres
e vertical interval is 5m

2 km or 1 mile
A249 Maidstone

The Kent Downs Area of Outstanding Natural Beauty near Coldharbour –

gently undulating pastoral scene.

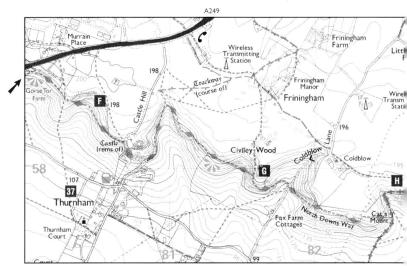

A249

Murrain Place

Friningham Farm

Wireless Transmitting Station

198

Trackway (course of)

Friningham Manor

Friningham

Gorse Tor Farm

F 198

Castle Hill

Castle (rems of)

Civiley Wood

Coldblow Lane

196

Coldblow

G

H

58

107

37

Thurnham

North Downs Way

Cat's Mount

Thurnham Court

Fox Farm Cottages

81

82

99

Contours are given in
The vertical interval

valley. Walk to the edge of the wood and take the steps down to the bottom of the valley. Climb towards two trees **F** then veer right past the trees to the fence. Turn right and follow the fence to a stile leading on to a narrow road. Turn right on to the road and follow the slightly sunken lane, bearing left. Where the road to Thurnham **38** turns sharp right, the route forks left. Cross the stile and enter the woodland. The road marks the edge of the earthworks of Thurnham Castle, a typical motte and bailey castle, of which only fragments of masonry remain though the bank gives an idea of its scale.

Continue straight on and the trees and scrub open out to a bank of grass and bramble. When you reach an arable field, turn right to walk along the lower edge of this field with another scrubby bank on your right. If you follow the line of the fence you will soon bear right and descend steps, then bear left and climb more steps. At the top, turn right. The path winds along a relatively flat section through more dense bramble and scrub and descends gently. Go down steep steps, then climb more steps, bearing right. At the top turn right **G** and start another gentle descent. Continue through scrub to a sunken lane. Cross the road and walk up the track on the other side. Climb again through scrub and woodland. At the top of the hill continue straight on. Scramble down a steep slope and turn left at the fence, then continue walking crossing two stiles before turning left on the track towards the farm.

102

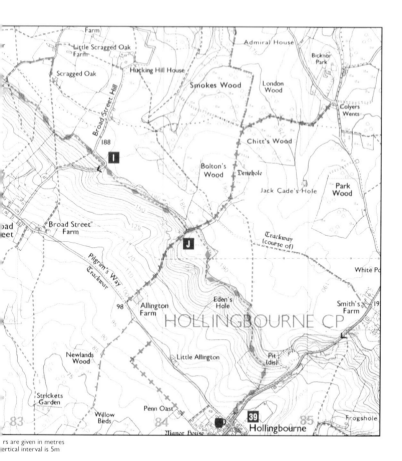

rs are given in metres
ertical interval is 5m

Bear right **H**, where a path leads left towards hidden farm buildings. Cross a stile and carry on up the hill. Cross a stile and emerge into a field, walk straight across to the wood. Walk through a narrow gap in the trees, emerge into a field, turn slightly left and walk to the far top corner of the field. Around to the left, cross a stile and bear right to the road **I**. Cross Broad Street and walk along the edge of the field, with a wire fence on the left, until you come to a stile leading into a woodland path. Turn left at the T-junction, go uphill for 50 yards (45 metres) before turning right. Pass a green metal barrier. Emerge on to the open downs and turn left through three more kissing gates as the well defined path descends down to Hollingbourne **39**. With the road now on your left, continue along the field-edge path and turn right at the road to reach the village.

A CIRCULAR WALK NEAR BOXLEY

3 miles (4.8 km)

While this is only a short walk, there is a steep ascent and descent in either direction and it can be very muddy in wet weather. If you are not already on the North Downs Way, a convenient starting point is by Boxley church **37**, which, in itself, merits a visit.

Look for a stile between the church lych gate and the entrance to Boxley House. Aim for the stile up the hill, keeping the open field on your right. Cross the next field diagonally, aiming for the stile in the top right-hand corner, then turn left and carry on towards the road, which you then cross. Follow the path as it steepens up the hill through the woods until you reach the main track of the North Downs Way. Turn right and follow the Way for about a mile (1.6 km) until you reach Hermitage Lane. Turn right and follow the lane downhill until you come to a crossroads with the road known as Pilgrims' Way. Turn left and immediately right into Harple Lane. After about 400 yards (365 metres), turn right on to a farm track by a cottage called East Lodge. Pass the turning left for Harpole Farm. After about half a mile (800 metres), the track bears left, but you cross a stile and head back towards the church, crossing another stile on the way.

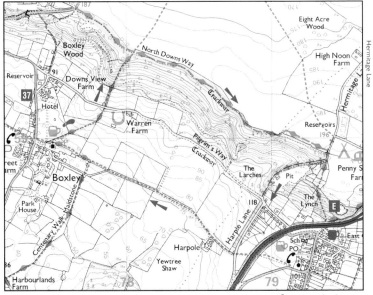

Contours are given in metres
The vertical interval is 5m

In Kent, concrete waymarks have traditionally been used to mark the Way, but now the familiar acorn is also used, as here near Detling.

8 Hollingbourne to Wye

past Harrietsham and through Boughton Lees
15 miles (24.1 km)

To continue on your way, at the crossroads by the Dirty Habbit pub, in Hollingbourne, you turn left along the narrow road keeping the pub on your right. After about half a mile (800 metres), the metalled lane bears round to the left and becomes a gravelly track, but your way continues straight on to a green road. This is the route of the old Pilgrims' Way, and it is quiet, pleasant, cross-country walking with easy going underfoot. Because it runs so straight, one cannot help thinking that it ought to have been a Roman road. There are now occasional concrete marker posts, to reassure you that you are still on the right route.

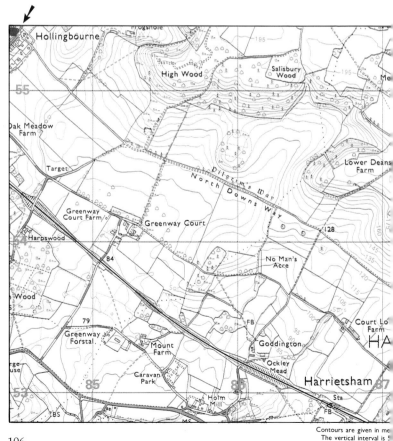

Contours are given in me
The vertical interval is 5

At a crossing of the ways, your route continues a little to the right on the broad dirt bridleway. Where the broad track seems to veer to the left into a field, your way should continue straight on, along a narrow woodland path heading gently uphill, and, as you ascend a little more steeply, the path becomes chalky underfoot.

Speedy walking this, and you soon arrive at the imposing white building, The Dutch House, where you continue straight on along the Pilgrims' Way, now metalled once more. At Pilgrim's Lodge, cross the road that leads down into Harrietsham to the right, and carry straight on – the Marley Works comes into view. To your right is the square tower of Harrietsham church. Keep straight on, passing the Marley Works and ignoring Flint Lane off to the left. Where the metalled road turns to the right, going down towards Lenham, your way continues straight on following the green lane.

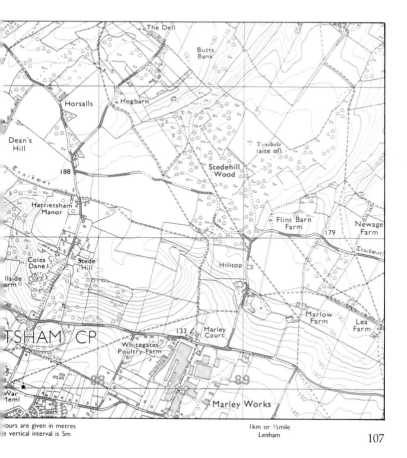

When you emerge on to the road, continue straight ahead and, at the next fork, bear left once again on to the Pilgrims' Way. Go through a gate and on to a broad drove road. Look out on the left for the war memorial cross, carved into the turf of the chalky hillside **40**, which commemorates the dead of the two world wars. The memorial stone was removed to the churchyard in 1960. The seat was presented to the people of Lenham by the Ashford Branch of the Community Association to commemorate their close links over the years. It offers a convenient place to take a break. Despite the proximity of the busy A20, this drove road makes for pleasant walking. Soon, go through another gate, to a hawthorn-hedged trackway.

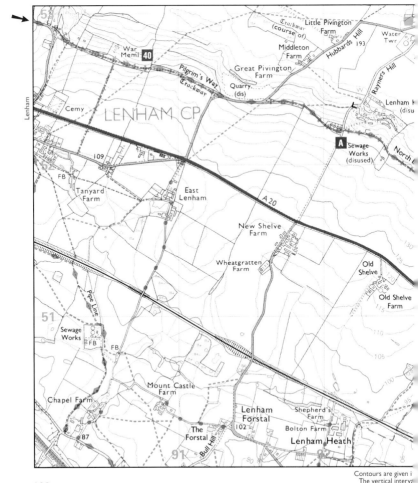

Contours are given i
The vertical interva

Bear left on to the road and, passing a field with chalk pits, where the road bears to the left, your route forks right on to another green lane. Dive into the tree-lined track, which soon emerges on to a metalled lane by some cottages. At the end of the row of cottages, turn left and immediately right **A**. Pass by the old sewage works, and the Way becomes a narrow field-edge path. At the large barns of Cobham Farm, continue on down the broad farm track. Where the track veers to the right, continue straight on across the field marked by a line of shrubbery and a bank. Pass through a gate by some trees and continue along the path. Near the top of the rise, go through another gate and carry straight on, passing what could be some fallen standing stones.

When you arrive at the minor road **B** near Hart Hill Farm, turn right and then after about 20 yards (18 metres), turn left on to another green bridleway. Pass beneath another quite old quarry working, and you can now see the houses of Charing,

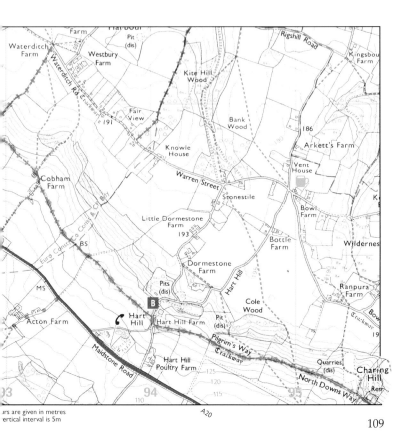

 urs are given in metres
ertical interval is 5m

with its square church tower. At an angled T-junction, the track forks right on to a dirt lane. At a large bungalow called Twyford you go straight on, keeping the bungalow to your right. Soon you arrive at the busy A252 by Reeves Cottage, where you turn left **C**, cross the road and continue into the lane on the right called Pilgrims' Way, which takes you past Burnt House Farm and Beacon Hill quarry into woodland.

Where the track emerges from the woodland it forks – your way continues on the left-hand fork, which is virtually straight onwards. The lane is metalled once again. When you come to an angled T-junction in the metalled lane, your route continues straight ahead, which is effectively left, and you can see the village of Westwell below you on the right. Carry on past the left-hand turning and pass an attractive flint-built cottage.

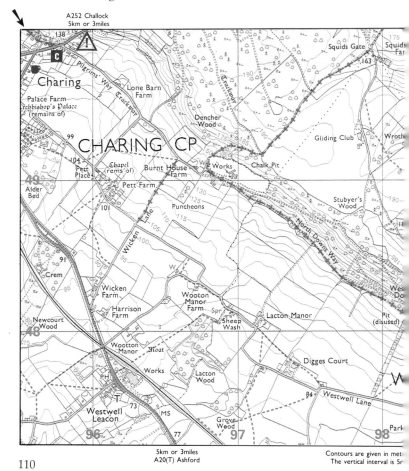

5km or 3miles
A20(T) Ashford

Contours are given in met
The vertical interval is 5r

You now come to the collection of houses, which is Dunn Street, where there is a postbox in the garden wall. The enterprising farmer has opened a campsite here. You then reach a T-junction, and your way continues straight across the road, on to a track and over a footpath into Eastwell Park. The National Trail crosses the field diagonally and you join a gravelled lane. The walking is easy now, as you crunch along the gravel drive. After a short ascent, by a corner of trees, the North Downs Way turns to the right, where the route straight ahead is marked 'Private Grounds' and 'Keep Out', and then turns immediately left by another corner of the trees. You are now walking along a chalky path, with cultivated land to your right and woodland to your left, making for a stile straight ahead.

Go over the stile and take the well-marked track diagonally across the arable field. Having crossed this stile, go across to another one and emerge on to a metalled lane with a church structure to your right. Your way continues straight along the road up the hill. This is the remains of St Mary's Church **41** by Eastwell Lake. A notice on the church says, 'This ancient house of God is being repaired by The Friends of Friendless Churches . . . It remains a consecrated building and the churchyard is sacred ground. Please respect them accordingly.' There is a fine flint building in the foreground.

At a T-junction in the lanes, go through a narrow kissing gate and walk along the right-hand side of the field by the

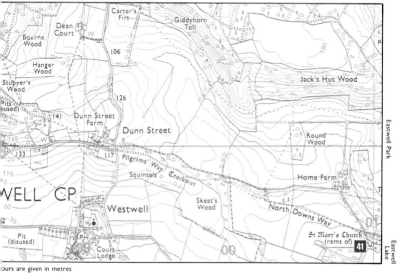

fence to a gate **D**. Just before the end of the tall line of trees that fringes the main estate driveway, the path veers down to the left and towards the drive and the stile. There is a tight-squeeze kissing gate on to the main driveway, where you turn right, and then you go through another kissing gate, and aim diagonally across the field ahead. Go through yet another narrow gate in the wall and on to the road. Cross the road diagonally to your left and join a lane. Fork right **E** at the 30 mph restriction sign.

You are now entering the village of Boughton Lees, and the village green and cricket ground are on your left, with the Flying Horse Inn opposite the green. Once past the village green, continue across the road into Pilgrims' Way and by Malt House farm, where a turning goes off to the left, continue straight on and up the hill a little. At the brow of the hill, you come to a point where you have to make a choice **F**. The North Downs way to Dover via Folkestone continues along the metalled lane, whereas the route via Canterbury turns left up a track (see pages 134–60).

To continue via Folkestone, where the road turns to the left, look out for the stile in the hedge on your right, indicating that you bear to the left. Walk parallel to the road along the field edge at first and then, by some cottages, turn right along the edge.

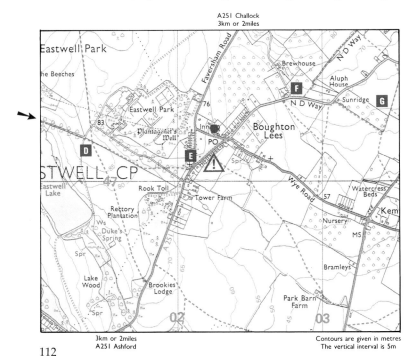

A251 Challock
3km or 2miles

3km or 2miles
A251 Ashford

Contours are given in metres
The vertical interval is 5m

To your left is a line of conifer trees. At the end of the trees, turn left and continue on the left-hand edge of the field, with an orchard behind the fence. The route continues across the fields but, after about 300 yards (275 metres), you need to look carefully for a right turning **G** to take you to the A28.

You reach the road by a pick-your-own farm. Turn left and walk parallel to the road and then cross to the right and go over another stile in a hawthorn hedge, and into an orchard. Walk down among the lines of apple trees, pass through a gap in the beech hedge and out on to Orchard Lane, effectively continuing straight on.

You now see Wye straight ahead. At the end of the old orchard, where the muddy track becomes grassy, turn right and then almost immediately left, keeping old strawberry beds to your left. This track is slippery and muddy after rain. Cross another stile and the railway is now in sight. Follow the well-defined path across the field to the road, passing across two more stiles. Go over the stile at the cattle grid on to the road and turn left. Turn right at the T-junction by Wye Station, cross the railway line and then cross the River Great Stour **42** by the road bridge. The attractive town of Wye offers most facilities, including pubs, restaurants, shops and accommodation.

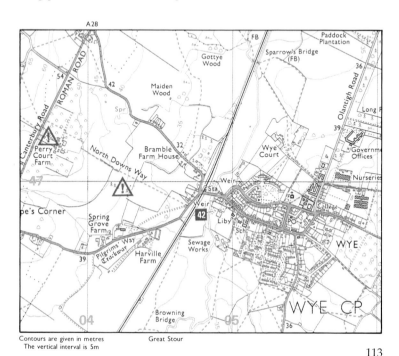

Contours are given in metres
The vertical interval is 5m

Great Stour

113

The natural history of chalk

Much of the higher ground that makes up the Surrey Hills and Kent Downs is underlain by chalk. Other National Trails, such as the South Downs and the Ridgeway, also follow the line of a chalk ridge. A glance at a simple geological map shows that much of south-eastern England is situated on chalk rock, which runs, like a three-pronged fork with a short handle, from the Dorset coast to north Norfolk, with the two southern tines separated by the Weald and meeting the sea via the North and South Downs. It is these well-drained chalk uplands that have been used as areas on which to farm, and on which lines of communication could be established away from the forested marshy and hostile lands in the valleys below.

Many people, if asked to describe chalk, might well name the white sticks used so commonly to write on school blackboards. In fact, chemically, this is a different material from that which is the foundation of chalk downland. On the other hand, most people have quite a good idea of typical chalk scenery with its rolling hills, springy, close-cropped turf, beech woodlands or wide-open arable land. But what is the chalk on which the land has evolved?

It has long been known that, chemically, chalk is largely calcium carbonate, so that it will effervesce in contact with an acid such as hydrochloric. Sometimes chalk may be stained reddish brown or yellowish orange with iron, and sometimes it is punctuated with layers of oddly shaped siliceous flints, but essentially chalk is white in colour so that, if the turf is removed to form, say, a giant crown shape on a hillside, the figure can be seen standing out white against green for miles around. It is permeable to water and, when soaked, can be soft and sticky, while, if it is dry, it seems as hard as any other stone. Its permeability to water allows the soils which form on it, shallow though they may be, to drain well. In fact, one of the problems with life on chalk country is the lack of permanent sources of water. It is this feature that led local people on some chalk downland areas to excavate the so-called dew ponds which are 'puddled' to make them waterproof.

It has also long been known that chalk must have formed as a sediment in the sea, but it was once thought to have been deposited in deep oceans because, in some ways, it resembles certain oozes that form in such places. It is now understood, however, that the great thickness of chalk which underlies the landscape was laid down in warm, shallow, clear seas, which spread across much of what is now northern Europe more than 65 million years ago. It was deposited as a very fine-grained, calcareous mud, which was made up largely of countless billions of tiny shells, shell fragments and the remains of some small plants called coccolithophorids. The tiny, calcareous plates are known as coccoliths. The flints that are so often found in the upper layers of chalk are made up of silica, but their exact origin remains uncertain. It may be that the compound that comprises them has resulted from a kind of 'gel' made from the solution of fragments of the skeletons of sea sponges.

Much of the Way follows the chalk escarpment and here, at Folkestone Warren Cliffs, the white rock is exposed, partly clothed in vegetation.

9 Wye to Etchinghill

past Stowting
11¼ miles (18.1 km)

Wye is home to Wye College, one of the country's leading agricultural institutions. To continue the route through the town, carry on up Bridge Street, passing the intriguing brick and wood building called The Swan's House, then turn left into Church Street almost opposite the Wife of Bath Restaurant. As its name suggests, Church Street is dominated by its typical Kentish, flint, square-towered church **43**, at the front of which is a North Downs Way information board. To the right of the church gate a sign tells you to fork right, keeping the church on your left.

Emerging from the churchyard, turn left on to a beech-hedged path by some allotments. At the end of the allotments, the path takes you right and then diagonally left by the Department of Biological Sciences into Occupation Road. Cross the road and continue up the lane which soon becomes a gravel track. From here you can just see the Crown Memorial **44** cut into the hillside but, as you approach the road, you get a much better view of it. Cross the road and head up the broad field path towards the trees.

Go over a stile and into the trees, continuing on uphill along the woodland path. At the top of the rise you meet a narrow lane, where you turn right **A**; there is a deep valley to your left. Continue to climb the hill and, where the route turns to the left, look for a rustic stile on the right, which takes you into the fields once more. Go over another stile and follow a field-edge path, keeping the line of trees to your right. Cross a stile and turn immediately left, walking along the edge of the downs with a fence on your left.

This is now lovely downland walking and long may it remain so. From here, you can just see the sea at last. The path simply follows the way indicated by the direction arrows, keeping between the edge of the downs itself and the fence on the left. The direction becomes obvious enough when you see a stile ahead. Cross the stile and follow the path, keeping the fence to the left.

All too soon, it seems, the trees obscure the view once more, as the Way continues through a field gate, where someone has thoughtfully laid concrete slabs for the times when the approach to the gate might be muddy. Turn right **B** on reaching the narrow road and, at the T-junction, cross the road and a stile into the Wye National Nature Reserve on Broad Downs **45** (see page 122). Cross the stile and you are on the open downland once more. Do not be misled by the arrow pointing to the right – follow the more obvious track, keeping the fence 10 or 15 yards (9–14 metres) on your right. Head towards a marker post, passing the deep, bowl-shaped hollow of the Devil's Kneading Trough **46** (see page 122). It is a spectacular cut, with trees in its base and a grassy bottom. This is downland walking at its best, especially on a fine summer's day with a cooling breeze blowing.

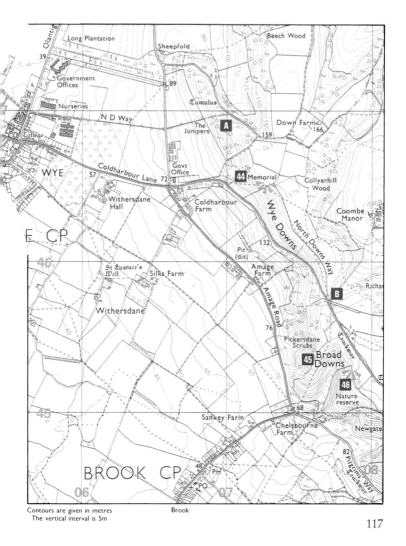

Contours are given in metres
 The vertical interval is 5m   Brook

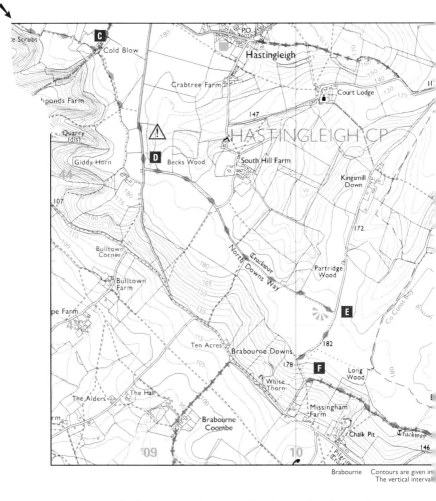

Brabourne   Contours are given in
                     The vertical interval

As you climb out of the trough, keep the fence line on
your left when crossing a stile. At the end of the field cross
a stile and skirt the boundaries of a kennels before crossing
another stile, heading towards Cold Blow Farm. By the farm
buildings **C**, go across three stiles into the open field once
more.

Keep to the right-hand edge of the field, following the line
of hawthorn trees and the fence. Cross another stile and then
take the obvious path across the arable field diagonally to the
left towards a gap in the hedge. Cross the stile and get on to
the narrow road, where you turn right. Take the next left-hand
turning **D** signposted to South Hill. Where the road bears left
to go to South Hill Farm, carry on along a green lane, which

then becomes a field-edge lane. You come to a metalled lane, where you turn right **E**.

Near the triangulation pillar, the lane bears to the left. Having descended for some distance, and where the lane bears to the right **F**, go through a gate on your left and up a farm track. Where the track forks, take the right fork and go through a gate on to a woodland-edge path.

You soon cross a narrow lane and continue on the way-marked track, now descending a little between hawthorn hedges. You quickly reach the road by a tall pylon where you turn left **G**, again downhill. Pass by Minnismore Stud and Saddlery, and carry straight on, past the telephone box. Soon after passing the house called Scotland, turn right across a stile in a gap in the hedge and follow a path parallel to the road across seven stiles, passing the Tiger Inn. In practice, like many others, you may choose to remain on the road, which is a quiet lane, rather than climbing all the stiles on this path – your energy will soon be needed. At the next fork at the post-box on the triangular green, bear left.

Before reaching the top of the hill on the lane, look out on your left-hand side for a turning off to the left **H**, uphill, on a narrow track. Soon, cross a lane, turn immediately left and immediately right on to another track. Climb Cobb's Hill, keeping the line of hawthorn trees and then the fence on your right. Effectively go straight on, by turning right and left over two stiles. Continue on across the next field, keeping the fence to your left. Cross another stile, following the field edge as it runs parallel to the road **I**.

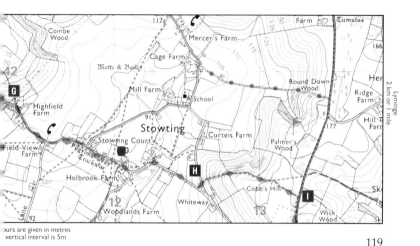

ours are given in metres
vertical interval is 5m

At the road junction **J**, cross straight over and walk parallel to the road; after passing a car park area look out for the left turn over a stile and go up stone steps to cross the road **K** and over another stile into the field, then follow the path, which effectively divides two fields. You can now clearly see ships ploughing up and down the Channel.

Follow the left-hand edge of the next field across a stile, and proceed more or less straight ahead to the left of the group of trees, into the dry valley, passing a small chalk working on your left. Follow the line of the valley, going under the pylons and passing between some trees to a clear waymarking post indicating a left turn up another sunken valley. At the top, turn sharp right **L** and follow the path as it contours the hill above Postling. Postling is a picturesque hamlet surrounded by apple orchards. Joseph Conrad lived in the village where he wrote some of his greatest novels, including *Lord Jim*, *Typhoon* and *Mirror of the Sea*. The church has an unusual dedication to St Mary and St Radegund: the latter was a sixth-century German priest and the church would originally have been linked to the twelfth-century St Radegund's Abbey 2 miles (4 km) west of Dover.

The track is well signed as it drops down towards the minor

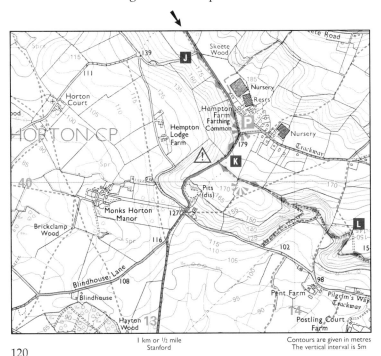

1 km or ½ mile
Stanford

Contours are given in metres
The vertical interval is 5m

road, where you turn left and, after 300 yards (275 metres), you reach the B2065 **M** at a stile. Cross the road, turning a little to the right, and then go up a narrow trackway between some trees. Pass over another stile, into the field, and continue on up the right-hand side of the field, heading roughly towards the radio mast. Once you reach this mast there are fine views in virtually every direction **47**. Bear to the left in front of the radio station and, by an old blackthorn tree, go over the stile to the right, keeping the fence of the radio station on your right. You soon go over another stile and on to the metalled drive to the radio station. Cross the drive diagonally to the right, and go over another stile. The tower is set on one of the highest points on the downs, at 595 feet (181 metres). It is a joint Civil Aviation Authority and Ministry of Defence air traffic radio site, known as Tolsford or Swingfield Station.

Walk between an avenue of old hawthorns through a military training area. Cross another stile a little to the left, and descend gently down a slightly muddy lane, which is clearly used as a cattle drove. Just before a stand of beech trees, turn sharp left over a stile and descend on the woodland-edge track. Emerge from the trees over a stile into the field, and continue along the left-hand edge of the field. Go over a stile, and you arrive at the road, which to the left leads you to Etchinghill. There is a welcome pub along the roadside before you reach the centre of the village.

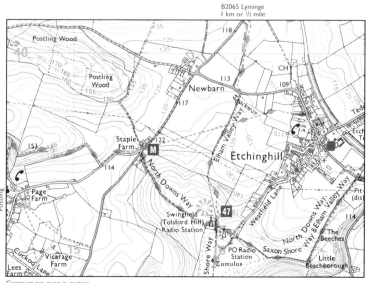

Contours are given in metres
The vertical interval is 5m

Wye Nature Reserve

Why Wye? The word *wye* seems to be of Saxon origin, meaning 'heathen temple', and dates from a time when Christianity was taking hold in Kent. Where the North Downs Way passes across Broad Downs and looks over the Devil's Kneading Trough, it takes you across the north-eastern edge of English Nature's Wye National Nature Reserve a mile or so to the east of Wye. While we might often think of open, rolling, chalk downland as a 'natural' habitat, it has been 'created', albeit over perhaps 2,000 years, by human use of the downs for grazing sheep. This environment, however, natural or not, was in balance for centuries and provided a home for many of our most important and attractive species of animals and plants.

During the early part of this century, sheep grazing declined and various scrubland plants, such as coarse grasses, hawthorn, blackthorn, dogwood, spindle, wayfarer's tree and privet, were able to invade, choking out the smaller and more fragile plants. Later, widespread ploughing of the downs, beginning with the Second World War's 'Dig for Victory' campaign, and the subsequent drive for Britain to be self-sufficient in food, left only a few small vital 'islands' of downland remaining, such as the 250 acres (100 hectares) of the Wye Reserve.

On the reserve, typically 'English' wild flowers such as cowslips and violets are common, as well as the prostrate, aromatic, wild thyme. The reserve boasts 17 species of orchids, as well as the more homely knapweed and ox-eye daisies, and this variety of plants attracts a myriad of butterflies and other insects. In turn, these provide food for a variety of birds, reptiles and small mammals, which may fall prey to the hovering kestrel. There are larger mammals here, too, such as fallow deer and badgers.

One notable geomorphological feature of the reserve is the deep cleft through the chalk, known as the Devil's Kneading Trough (there is a restaurant of the same name by the side of the road nearby). This coombe is a dry valley, which owes its origins to a time, some 10,000 years ago at the end of the last Ice Age, when the ground was more or less permanently frozen during winter. In spring, when a thaw set in, the meltwater washed from the hills fragments of chalk that had been shattered from the parent rock by frost action. Over about 500 years the deep, steep-sided gulley was formed.

The deep gully of the Devil's Kneading Trough took about 500 years to be carved by detritus-rich meltwaters some 10,000 years ago.

Without careful management, scrub would soon take over, and selective clearing and grazing are used to control invaders. Similarly, to maintain the traditional woodland, trees are thinned and coppiced, and diseased specimens are cut down, sometimes to be left as habitats for fungi, insects and other small creatures.

10 Etchinghill to Dover

via Folkestone
12 miles (19.3 km)

To continue from the point at which you crossed the road leading down to Etchinghill, turn right **A**, and fork immediately left
down a 'No Through Road'. Descend the lane and turn second
left on to a track. Go over a stile and into a field. Make for the
corner of the field, where you can just see a stile; then cross
this on to a woodland path. Go over a plank bridge. Where the
path divides, take the left-hand fork going under the railway
bridge and pylons. Head on up the steep climb through the
attractive sheep-grazed valley **48**.

Continue upwards, making for the acorn mark that you can
just see between two groups of hawthorns. Turn right **B** and
follow the fence on your left. Go over another stile and turn
left, keeping along the left-hand edge of the field. At the next
field corner turn right, making for the next gap in the fence.

Keep on the left-hand side of the field, with the fence to your
immediate left. The path forks in the middle of the field, and
the National Trail takes the left fork. Go left around the corner

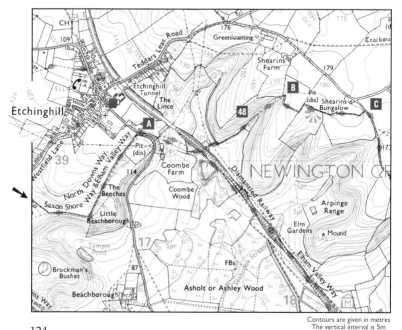

Contours are given in metres
The vertical interval is 5m

124

of the field, and head for a stile, where you turn right **C** on to a sunken lane, which remains wet even in dry weather. Follow the fence- and bramble-lined track until you arrive at a lane. Cross this and go over the stile into the next field, turning immediately right. Then walk down the right-hand edge of the field. You can now see the outskirts of Folkestone below you.

Follow the field edge round until you come to a kissing gate where you turn right and follow the track under the bank and join a very obvious path. Enter a basin of chalk known as Pene Quarry, and climb some steps to continue on the cliff-edge path. Simply follow the waymarks and, where necessary, the stiles, passing by the odd concrete pillbox until you reach a road. Up on the escarpment the air is good, the sea is attractive, the walking feels airy, and from here you can definitely see the coast of France across the Channel providing that the day is a clear one; almost beneath your feet are the marshalling yards and loading ramps of the Channel Tunnel terminal.

Cross the road and get back on to the clifftop path again, then use a newly designed kissing gate. It is good to have reached the sea, even if you are separated from it by Folkestone and developments including, of course, the Folkestone Terminal of the Channel Tunnel. Emerge from the grazing area through another kissing gate to continue, following the roadside track, passing through another kissing gate and into the trees. You

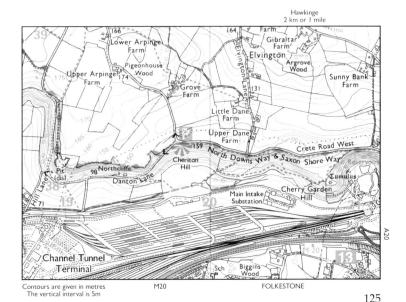

Contours are given in metres
The vertical interval is 5m

soon see the obvious earthworks known as Caesar's Camp **49**. Turn right along the path to the hill and cross over it, bearing left to a point near the road again before bearing right, around Round Hill, to a layby near the main road. Turn right and cross the A260 from Crete Road West and continue on up the hill on Crete Road East. A couple of hundred yards (180 metres) up the hill on the right, opposite a bungalow, a stile takes you into a field and onto a path running parallel to the road.

At the staggered crossroads, cross two stiles to carry straight on in the same direction, over the road and into the next field. Look out for the triangulation pillar **50** of Dover Hill on your right, standing at 558 feet (170 metres). You soon arrive at the

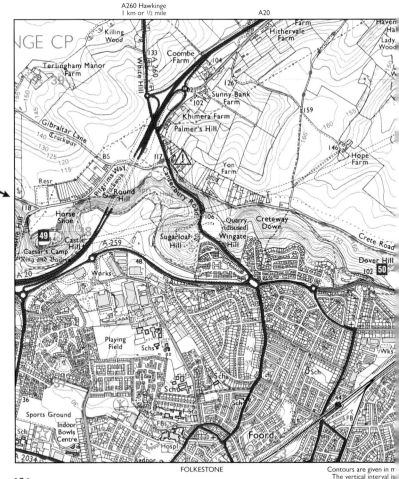

FOLKESTONE

busy B2011 trunk road opposite the Valiant Sailor public house, where you turn right. Cross the road towards the Valiant Sailor and follow the footpath signposted to The Warren **51**, Eastcliff and Dover just to the right of the pub. Folkestone Warren, an area of rough grass and scrub at the foot of the cliffs and separated from the sea by the railway line that links Folkestone and Dover, is an area of great interest to naturalists; it provides a home to several rare species of plants.

Walk to the cliff edge, with a caravan site on your left, turn left, keeping the coast on your right. All along the Way here there are temptations to descend the cliffs, but stay on the cliff edge, passing the Battle of Britain memorial, a cliff-top café and another caravan park.

urs are given in metres
vertical interval is 5m

In front of a big white house, bear left with the track, cross a stile and turn right up the track once more to the cliff-edge path signposed to Abbot's Cliff House.

Go through a gate and walk to the right of a bunker which marks the site of a disused rifle range, go through another kissing gate back onto the cliff edge. There have been numerous cliff falls in this area due to water weakening the chalk cliffs. This, understandably, causes concern to local property owners. Inevitably, one day it will all fall into the sea; in the

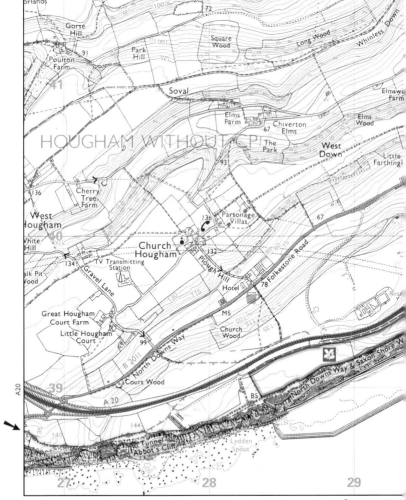

Contours are given i
The vertical interva

meantime, engineers continue to buy time. Some recent falls have caused problems for the National Trail's managers, as the legal line of the path was left running through space and the authorities had to negotiate a revised definitive line along the new cliff edge.

Having passed the rifle range, you simply follow the cliff-edge path, walking over the top of Shakespeare Cliff to Aycliffe, where the outskirts of Dover and the approaching end of your journey are marked by a creatively sculpted seat.

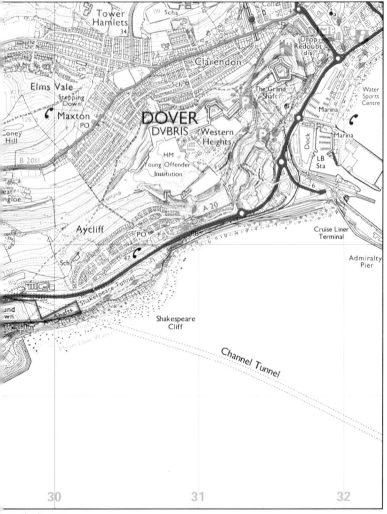

At the end of the allotment area, having descended the cliff, turn left and go through the underpass and right at the other side. Turn first left among the houses along King Lear's Way and right into King's Ropewalk. Shakespeare Cliff owes its name to the scene in *King Lear* in which the blind Earl of Gloucester attempts to leap off the precipice, and there are many other Shakespearean place names hereabouts. At the end of the close bear left up some steps and turn right through a kissing gate to cross the meadow, turning right onto the road.

At the T-junction turn left by the garage and follow the path down the hill. As the road bears to the right look out for a kissing gate and a flight of steps up to the hill to the right which skirts the left-hand edge of the fort. This area, known as Western Heights, has long been a key part of Dover's fortifications.

Turn left before the kissing gate and go down the steps through the gate to the road. Turn right and follow the road as it bears to the left to the busy main road. Turn left and cross York Street at the lights. Walk straight down Queen Street. Turn left onto King Street and you will come to the Market Square: you have reached the end of your walk.

High above the town, Dover Castle stands guard and contains within its perimeter a Roman lighthouse and a Saxon church.

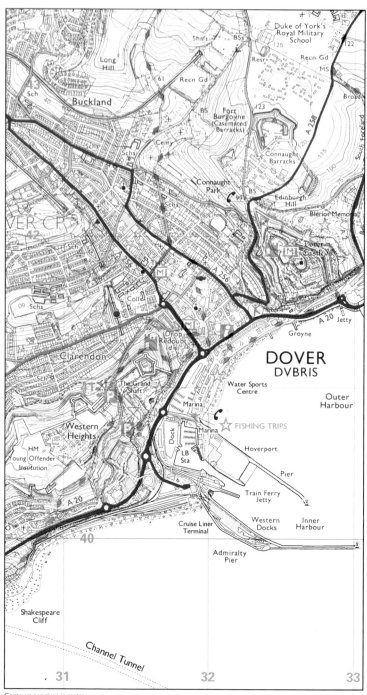

DOVER
DVBRIS

Duke of York's Royal Military School

Fort Burgoyne (Casemated Barracks)

Connaught Barracks

Edinburgh Hill

Blériot Memorial

Dover Castle

Connaught Park

Long Hill

Buckland

Clarendon

Western Heights

HM Young Offender Institution

Drop Redoubt

The Grand Shaft

Water Sports Centre

Outer Harbour

★ FISHING TRIPS

Marina

Dock

Marina

LB Sta

Hoverport

Pier

Train Ferry Jetty

Western Docks

Inner Harbour

Cruise Liner Terminal

Admiralty Pier

Shakespeare Cliff

Channel Tunnel

Jetty

Groyne

A 20

A 256

A 258

South Foreland

Contours are given in metres
The vertical interval is 5m

Near Boughton Aluph the North Downs Way, here a footpath, hastens arrow

straight across the arable land.

11 Boughton Lees to Canterbury

through Chilham and Chartham Hatch
13 miles (20.9 km)

For the northern route of the North Downs Way via Canterbury, after going through Boughton Lees (see page 112), about half a mile (800 metres) up the lane, turn left **F** as indicated. Go through a narrow, fence-lined path with fields to left and right. The track bears left and right round the field.

As you emerge from a tunnel of blackthorn and hawthorn, there is a tall beech hedge on your right and the low, solid-looking, square-towered church of Boughton Aluph comes into view. Before you get to the church, go through a gate **A** and into a meadow, and walk round its left-hand edge. At the end of the meadow, go over a stile in front of the church, and on to a lane, which you cross and then continue on the same line into the next field over a stile. Keeping the farm buildings on your left, make for a gate in the fence and a trackway beyond, then go over a complicated-looking stile and gate, and down the pathway beneath the fields. When you approach the road, follow the track as it bears left and right, and go through a little cutting and on to the road by a house.

Cross the road, turning left and immediately right towards Soakham Farm along the gravelled drive. Continue straight through Soakham Farm, keeping the farmhouse on your left and a barn on your right, and pass on up the track through a gate. Continue to follow the farm track as it zigzags towards the trees up the hill. You soon have your first ascent of the day, as you climb up towards the trees on the sunken track. At the edge of the trees, go through a gate and continue up the narrow woodland-edge track. You are rising on to Soakham Downs. A sculpture has been carved into the chalk here, offering sheltered seating in the form of a sheep scrape.

Just before you come to the end of the trees, the track turns to the right, and you are now walking just beneath the top of the ridge with the woodland on your right. Shortly afterwards the path forks yet again **B** and your route follows the left-hand option.

This is young sweet chestnut woodland. At a crossing of the ways, in a clearing, continue straight on along the narrow path, but where the track forks again, you go left. At an angled T-junction in the woodland ways, a hidden marker post tells you to go effectively straight on and not turn left, and you continue to follow a north-north-easterly line along the ridge of the Downs.

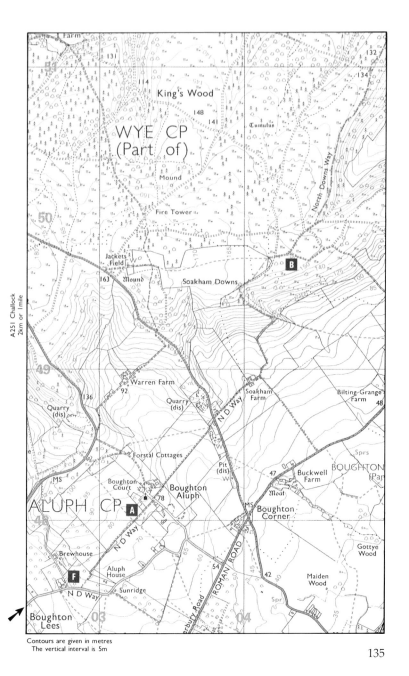

Contours are given in metres
The vertical interval is 5m

After perhaps half an hour of walking, the trees thin out on your right and then, at another angled T-junction in the tracks, turn right – effectively straight on. A Forestry Commission notice tells you that you are leaving King's Wood and, at a crossing of the ways, an acorn marker points you straight on along the edge of the woodland; do not turn right over the stile or turn left into any of the other trackways into the woods. At the next junction **C** turn right, downhill a little.

You are now descending out of the trees and looking towards wooded parkland. To the right there is the fine brick house of Godmersham Park **52**. At a T-junction in the tracks **D** continue left; do not go through the gate to the right.

When you arrive at a kind of angled T-junction with a narrow, partly metalled, partly gravelly lane, your way continues straight on. You are now walking around the edge of the grounds of Chilham Park **53**. Walk on down the metalled avenue, past the houses known as Mountain Street, and the lake that is owned by the private Chilham Fishing Club.

Where the road forks, take the left fork uphill a little – and walk beneath a high brick wall, passing St Mary's Church of England Primary School on your right, until you arrive at Chilham. Walk across the attractive little square towards the 15th century White Horse public house and the church **54**, and then into the churchyard. Continue past the solid-looking, flint-built St Mary's church and veer a litttle away from the churchyard on a path to the left, where you go through a gate and down a track. You emerge on to a narrow lane to continue straight ahead towards the more major road.

Go straight across the A252 on to the next path, signposted to Selling, and at the next crossroads in the minor lanes, go straight on up the hill, signposted to Old Wives Lees. The path is off the road to the left for 330 yards (300 metres). At a complicated set of crossings **E**, bear half right into Pilgrims' Way and pass the post office and North Court Oast.

Oast houses, their ventilation cowls adding an unusual outline to farmsteads in this hopping area, are buildings to house the oasts or kilns for drying newly picked hops, 'oast' having once been the word for a kiln of any kind. The revolving cowls of the oast house adjust the draught to the wind, helping to draw the heat up from the oasts through and around the hops. In 1574 the Kentish squire, Reginald Scot, described the complexities of growing, poling, picking and drying over the 'oste', in his *Perfite platforme of a Hoppe Garden*.

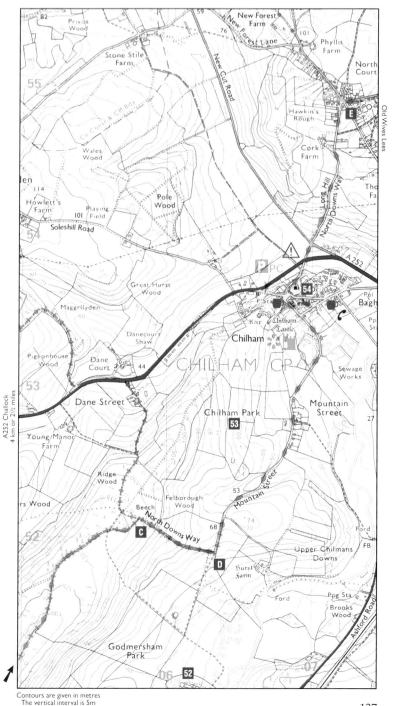

Contours are given in metres
The vertical interval is 5m

137

At the fork, bear left. Immediately afterwards at the next point of the triangle, turn right and then immediately left, over a stile and walk between the lines of trees. At the bottom of the track, go through a kissing gate and on to a field path down towards a lane. At the corner of a hop field, turn right on to the gravelled lane and after about 10 yards (9 metres), by a line of trees, turn left, following the trees uphill.

When you reach the top of the rise, the track bears to right and left. Turn sharp left **F** at the fence in front of the orchard and walk around the edge of the orchard on your right for about 150 yards (135 metres). Turn right and go over a stile into the orchard itself, walk down the left-hand side and, at a crossing in the orchard tracks, go right and immediately left.

At the end of the orchard, where the track bears to the right, do not miss the metal fence and stile **G** over the railway line. Cross another stile and turn right up the lane, continuing round to your right, and then left on the metalled orchard lane, keeping some oast houses to your left. Throughout this section there are scattered idyllic, secluded properties set among the orchards. Although they give the impression of being isolated and totally rural, the City of Canterbury is less than 4 miles (6 km) away. At a crossroads, look for a marker post beneath an old pine, which points up a track with a hedge to your right. At the top of the rise, where you meet a concrete lane, turn left on to this lane. Where the concreted and then tarmacked lane bears round

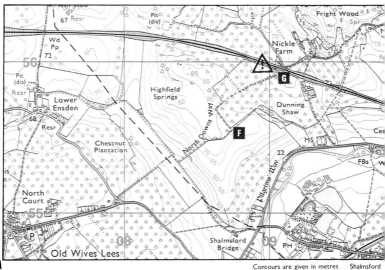

Contours are given in metres   Shalmsford
The vertical interval is 5m

to the left, go straight on, or fork right on to the older, rougher lane heading towards three oast houses and a radio tower.

At some farm buildings, turn left and immediately right on to a well-kept gravelled lane. You arrive at the lane by Hoppers Farmhouse Bakery **55** and turn left and immediately right into New Town Street to enter the village of Chartham Hatch **56**.

You arrive at the junction from New Town Street and the route bears to the left and then, when Nightingale Close bears to the right, continues straight across on to a narrow fence-lined path. Carry on across the road down a track. Where the track forks turn right towards a recreation field. Walk down its right side, with a fence and houses on your right, and on to a path that descends into woodland. You will emerge into an orchard and, on your left, you can see the busy A2. Towards the end of the newer part of the orchard, turn left **H** on a sandy path and then follow the waymark posts through the woods. At a T-junction in the tracks, turn right in front of a hop field. When you arrive at a metalled concrete road by a fence **I**, turn right and immediately left on to a road. Cross the dual carriageway and turn right. Near the top of the hill, go straight on, and not over the stile, follow the track round to the left where it becomes gravelled.

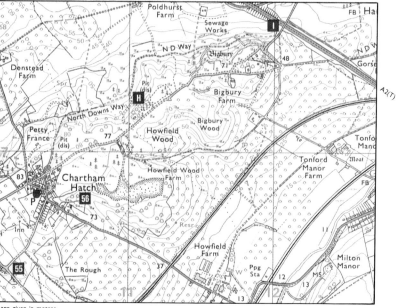

are given in metres
tical interval is 5m

Go over a little footbridge and up the track. You emerge onto a driveway at Hindora Heights and bear left, effectively straight on, and continue along the metalled lane, ignoring any footpaths to your right or left. The land on the left, known as Golden Hill, is owned by the National Trust. The trackway here is often scattered with scallop shells, the symbols of St James of Compostella, which are carried by the pilgrims who continue to make their way to the shrine of the martyred archbishop, Thomas à Becket. Where the lane forks, with a cycleway going off to the left, your way bears to the right. Emerge into the traffic **J** by some houses and you arrive at a roundabout.

At the end of Mill Lane cross Knight Avenue and take the underpass to the left to cross the busy A2050 Rheims Way and walk along London Road to the church of St Dunstans. Turn right here onto St Dunstans Street, cross the River Stour and turn left in the main shopping area down Mercery Lane to reach the West Gate to the Cathedral **57**.

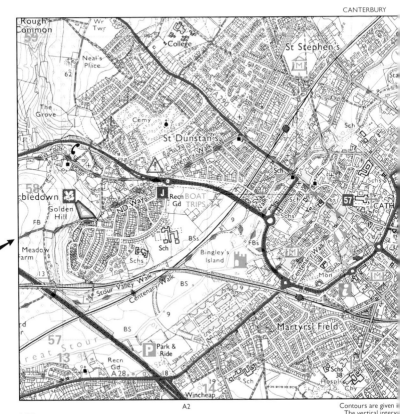

A2

Contours are given in
The vertical interva

Canterbury and the pilgrims

Encouraging their mounts to make more haste, horseriders along the North Downs Way symbolise in their language an early connection with pilgrims to the cathedral city, for the word 'canter' is an abbreviation of 'Canterbury gallop', the gentle galloping pace at which medieval devotees approached their destination.

In some ways, and especially to 14th century critics of the whole idea of pilgrimage, as it was then practised, there is another connection between today's holidaymakers along the Way and the pilgrims of Chaucer's day. Modern visitors to many tourist centres, including Canterbury, may proclaim the fact of their visit by wearing T-shirts or displaying badges on rucksack or car. While travellers of the 1300s may not have worn T-shirts or driven cars, they could certainly buy badges to demonstrate their devotion and prove that they had made their pilgrimage to Canterbury and to the shrine containing the remains of the martyred Archbishop, Thomas à Becket. The most common image on such badges was the scallop of Compostella, an image that is still associated with Pilgrims' Way road signs.

Travellers leaving Canterbury on the North Downs Way heading for Dover will pass close to St Martin's Church, which claims to have the oldest origins of any church in Britain. It was built in AD 560 on the site of a Roman church of the 1st century. Canterbury, however, is the seat of the archbishopric established by St Augustine, the Roman monk who headed the group of missionaries that landed in England in AD 597 with the aim of converting the English to Christianity.

While, today, Canterbury Cathedral is the Mother Church of the Anglican Communion, before the Reformation the Archbishop would have been a Roman Catholic, originally elected by the monks from among their brotherhood, and later an outsider granted the title by the king as a mark of favour. Like most of England's cathedrals, the great church of Canterbury was rebuilt shortly after the Norman Conquest. Originally, there was also a Benedictine priory here, which fell foul of Henry VIII's dissolution of the monasteries, following his break with Rome in 1534. Not least of Henry's aims at Canterbury was to get his hands on the huge quantity of treasure that medieval pilgrims had placed here. One consequence was that the shrine to Thomas à Becket, which had stood since 1220

Hop fields with their supporting frameworks near Old Wives Lees. Lines of trees, like those in the background, were once used to provide shelter.

where Trinity Chapel is now, was demolished. On the south side of the cathedral the flight of stone steps, still called the Pilgrim Steps, remains to mark the approach to the shrine.

The Kentish hop fields

The hop is a climbing plant of the genus *Humulus,* which probably once grew wild in the wet woodlands of southern England. It is a common hedgerow plant today, but usually as a result of escapes from commercial hop gardens. It is the female flower, or 'cone', of the hop that is used to give the bitter flavour and 'hoppy' aroma to bitters, lagers, milds and stouts; it also helps to clarify and preserve the beer. In England, it was probably during the 16th century that hops were first used for this purpose and this was when commercial hop fields were established. Before that, English 'ales' would have been flavoured with honey or herbs.

The Kentish hop fields of today owe their origins to the system set up in the late 19th century, when permanent structures of uprights, wirework and strings were first used as the framework for the hops to entwine. Before that, various structures of poles were used, based on the methods used in Flanders. In the same way that the climate allows Kent to be an important fruit-growing area, hops also need plenty of sunlight and a mild climate. To protect the hop plants from strong winds, the fields were traditionally sheltered by lines of poplars or by thin hedges – still a feature of the landscape in some areas. Today, however, screens of coarse netting are usually used. It is interesting to note that continental lagers are hopped with female flowers that have not been fertilized by the males while, in England, no particular effort is made to exclude the male flowers from the gardens.

Hops are usually picked in August and although, today, this is usually carried out by machine, it was once a manual operation and, as well as the local farm workers, itinerant hoppers, such as gypsies and holiday makers from London, would arrive in Kent in large numbers for the season.

A CIRCULAR WALK FROM CHILHAM

4¾ miles (7.6 km)

Leave Chilham Square by Chantry Cottage and carry on down the hill past the post office. Bear left by the Woolpack Inn, past the next turning on your right and continue to follow this minor road until you cross the A28 Ashford road by the garage. Go over the railway and then use the footbridges to cross the Great Stour. After the second bridge, follow the path in front of the brick cottage and on up the hill through the woods. Cross another stile, carry on into a field and then turn left to follow the left-hand hedge. Where the hedge turns to the left, head rightish towards the woodland, where you then turn left and follow the track for just over a mile (2 km) until you reach a minor road.

Rustling underfoot is a constant accompaniment as you walk through this woodland avenue near Old Wives Lees.

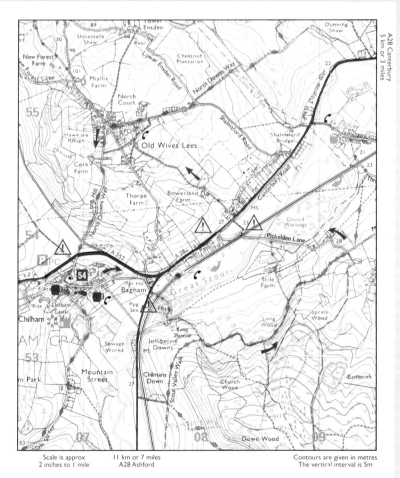

Scale is approx
2 inches to 1 mile

11 km or 7 miles
A28 Ashford

Contours are given in metres
The vertical interval is 5m

Once there turn left and follow this lane for just under a mile (1.3 km) until you arrive at the A28 once more, crossing the Great Stour and the railway again on the way. Turn right, cross the road, and then turn left into Bowerland Lane and head for Bowerland Farm. Through the farm, continue on between a large field and an orchard, go through the gate, and follow the path to the road. Turn left and walk into Old Wives Lees, passing the post office and shop on your left. You have now joined the North Downs Way once again. At the four-way road junction, take the second left towards Chilham. Walk down the hill for about two-thirds of a mile (1 km) and go straight across at the first crossroads, and straight across at the next. Just up the hill, fork left through the churchyard to get back to the picturesque square in the centre of the village.

145

12 Canterbury to Dover

via Patrixbourne and Shepherdswell
18¾ miles (30.2 km)

Our route out of Canterbury starts at the West Gate to the Cathedral **57**. Here you turn right and cross the ring road at Burgate continuing down Church Street and turning right at St Pauls along Moncestry Street, keeping the wall of St Augustine's Abbey on the left **A**. Follow the path at the side of the road signed to Littlebourne and Sandwich on the A257. Just past the turning on your left towards St Martin's Church **58** turn right down Spring Lane **B** and right again into Pilgrims Way. At St Augustines Road continue straight ahead and turn right continuing along the Pilgrims Way across the railway and on to the end of the residential area. There is much to see in Canterbury and visitors rarely do it justice on a single visit. As you walk out of the city towards the south, do not forget to look back and admire

No visit to Canterbury is complete without visiting the city's magnificent cathedral, rebuilt shortly after the Norman Conquest.

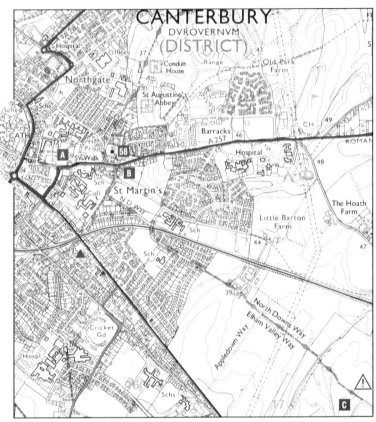

Contours are given in metres
The vertical interval is 5m

the view which, for many, is their first sight of the city and
the great cathedral that dominates it.

Pass through the buildings of Little Barton storage depot, and
continue on along the metalled way. At a crossing in the lanes,
go straight on along the track which is also signposted Cycle
Route 16. East Kent has ambitious plans for extending its cycle
routes and linking them into the planned national network.

After a second row of pylons, just into the trees, the lane
forks, and your way continues left up the hill, whereas the
right-hand fork goes into an orchard. In a short distance your
lane also enters orchard country. Where you join another road
at an angled T-junction C, continue straight on, past Hode
Oast Cottage and a little brick cottage.

You soon arrive at a minor, but quite busy, road where, at
an angled T-junction, you turn left – effectively straight on at

the mini-roundabout. Your way continues straight down a road signposted to Patrixbourne, heading for where you can just see a postbox.

You pass a white-painted gatepost with some remarkable topiary box trees in the front in the shape of a helter-skelter. Topiary, the art of trimming and training trees or bushes into artificial decorative animal, geometric or other shapes, was an art known to the Egyptians and Romans and has always exercised a strong influence on European gardens. Box edging, in particular, has always been viewed as a kind of outdoor embroidery – equally versatile as a simple hedge around a herb bed or for edging paths in a kitchen garden.

Walk down through the village of Patrixbourne, passing an entrance to the Old Vicarage. At the fork in the roads, turn right, aiming towards the fine, flint-built Church of St Mary's **59**, one of the lovely churches to be found in the area. Then pass the front of the Old Vicarage. Go over a little bridge and just past a house called Cherry Trees, and then look for a track located to your left **D**. Cross the field diagonally towards the trees, then follow the path round to the right towards the A2.

At a corner of the woods, bear left and up the field-edge path. Where the path seems almost to topple into the A2 road cutting, go through a gate and bear left on to a woodland path and walk beside the A2 for some distance. You now have an orchard on your left (for more information on the orchards of Kent see page 158).

You eventually come to a metalled driveway, where there is a bridge over the A2; this leads back into the village of Bridge, now restored to relative tranquillity after being by-passed. Cross the driveway and continue straight on to the track once more; go through a gate on your left and follow the obvious track before you, aiming towards a clump of trees.

As you reach the trees, veer to the right **E** and continue on the path, keeping the trees on your left. Where the track seems to disappear to the left into the orchard, continue straight on the field-edge path with a high hedge on your left. Cross the road and go through a gate, follow the footpath across the big field, heading a little to the right towards the road.

Stay with the path as it veers a little to the left and then continues parallel with the trunk road.

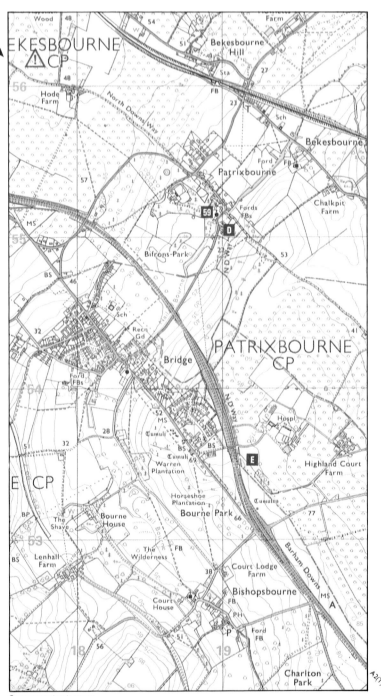

Contours are given in metres
The vertical interval is 5m

149

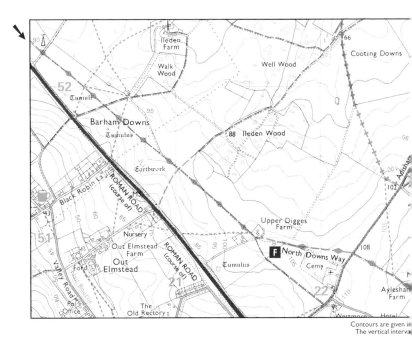

Contours are given in
The vertical interval

After crossing the huge field, cross the metalled lane and
continue on, and into, the next field, where there is a
well-marked path. Go through the kissing gate at the gap
in the hedge, across the concrete lane, and into the next
huge field.

Aim diagonally left, away from the road, to meet a track
between the fields. Turn right onto the track and pass
several posts that direct you towards the farm. Where the
main track bears to the left at the farm, continue straight
on and skirt the house to the right. At a gravel track turn
left, bear right through a gate and at the next farm track
turn right by the barn, following the line of telegraph poles.

Veer left **F** at the end of the hedgerow on your left towards the
two telegraph poles near the road. When you arrive at the road,
cross over it. The route now seems to follow the line of the telegraph poles towards a hedge, some trees and, beyond, some
houses. Continue into Womenswold **60** along the left-hand side
of the field by two old willow trees. The church is on your right.

After about 10 yards (9 metres) you arrive at a farm track
with a corrugated-iron barn on your right. Continue down the
land until you reach the unspoilt old village. Turn left and
immediately right, going down the gravel track, passing

Nethersole House on your left. Continue straight on ignoring the footpath to the left. Continue straight on ignoring the footpath to the left. You soon arrive at a narrow lane, which you cross, going straight ahead into a woodland path.

You emerge from the woods onto another lane, where you turn right. Just before you reach the crossroads, look for a stile on the left-hand side of the road **G**, which you cross, and go down the field-edge path to your right. Cross a stile on your right into the green and cross another to follow a field-edge path parallel to the road. In contrast to the sleepy hamlet of Womenswold, the village here is a relatively recent settlement, built for workers at the nearby Elvington pit. At the bottom of the hill cross a stile on the right and turn left on the road. Where road bears round to the left, continue straight on up the hill on the green lane. You are now rising onto Three Barrows Down **61**, the tumuli can be seen in the wood at the top of the 339-foot (103-metre) hill.

As soon as you get to the top, you start descending gently once more, and then start to climb towards the railway. As you reach the railway, fork right on to a broader track and then, where that meets a metalled lane, turn left to cross the lines and immediately afterwards, at the next junction, turn right, signposted to Eythorne and Waldershare.

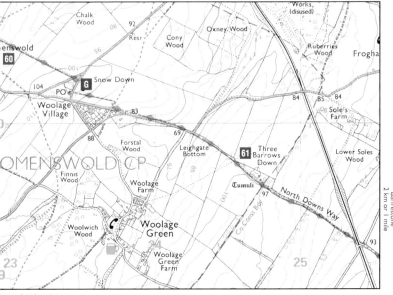

rs are given in metres
ertical interval is 5m

Near Womenswold in late summer, fields of ripening maize and wheat proclaim Kent's role as more than the 'Garden of England'.

Pass by the buildings of Long Lane Farm, and continue up the lane. By Long Lane Cottage, turn right **H** on to what at first is a grassy drive just past the entrance to the cottage. Go through the kissing gate, and continue along the grassy drove road. At the end of this, go through another kissing gate, and on to the road by a junction. Turn right, cross the old railway line and look for a gate on your left. Go through the gate, and follow the obvious path.

You are now cutting through the outskirts of Shepherdswell, and you pass a post with a plaque on top of it in memory of Ronald C. Clark, Parish Councillor 1955–88. There is bed and breakfast accommodation to be found here as well as shops.

Having passed the memorial post on council property, go through another kissing gate and on to a gravelly lane. Cross the lane and continue in the same direction towards a gate and stile, which you cross to follow the obvious right of way across the field towards the next stile. Continue on up the hill towards a telegraph pole with some houses to the left of it. To your right there is a playing field behind the hedge. Go through the gate and carry on up the gravelly drive, a stable block on the right, then go through a kissing gate and on to a pathway. Cross the pathway, and continue on to the path facing you. This is a residential lane.

You soon arrive at a road, where you turn right and, just after Upton House, left, through a kissing gate **I**. Continue down the track, passing a churchyard with an attractive little church on the right **62**. It is said that the church was built as a thanks offering by a nobleman who nearly lost his life in the forest. It is very small and without a tower of any kind. The bell hangs from a yew tree in the churchyard. Go over another stile and follow the left-hand edge of a meadow, with farm buildings on your right. Cross into the field on your left, and walk down the right-hand side of the field. At the bottom, go through a gap in the hedge and bear slightly left **J** across the field to the point where a line of trees comes to the hedge bank. Go over a stile and continue on the same line through the next field and up over a hill.

A chimney comes into view through the trees, and you should be aiming to the left of the buildings of Coldred Court Farm to emerge by the church. Turn right on the metalled lane to the crossroads. At the crossroads follow the footpath into the trees – effectively straight on and to the left. Soon the path emerges from the trees into a field where you carry straight on to a clump of beech trees. You can just about make out the line of the path in the fields on the other side. Keep to a line which leaves the three small clumps of trees and a water tower to the right.

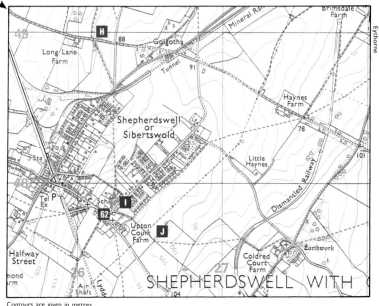

Contours are given in metres
The vertical interval is 5m

When you reach a farm track by the corner of some trees, go over a stile and aim diagonally across the fields to the left and locate another stile. You are now walking across the typically grassy meadows near Waldershare House **63**, a fine, 18th-century, brick-built manor house. Continue through the next field, crossing a track, to the next stile. Carry straight along the metalled track down the hill and, at a crossing of the driveways, turn left towards a yellowish house. Emerge through a gate, by the house and a T-junction in the lane, where you turn right.

When the drive reaches a crossroads **K**, look for a marked route between the fork, going straight ahead. Go through the circular clump of trees via an iron kissing gate, and out into a meadow, following the obvious path towards another gate in another band of trees. Go right over a stile and right through a wrought-iron gate into a courtyard of a little flint-built church **64**. Pass through the lynch gate and turn right on to the church lane.

At the end of the lane turn right and walk along the road, taking the first left to cross the A256 on a bridge. At the other side, turn left down a concrete track to Minacre Farm. Go over the stile and bear half right **L** just before the farm. Cross another stile and head up the hill towards a finger-post and some trees on the horizon. Do not continue on the farm track. Go over a stile, up a step or two and on to a narrow road, where you turn left and follow this road as it bears down to the right. You are now in the village of Ashley and, where the road turns sharply to the left, you should

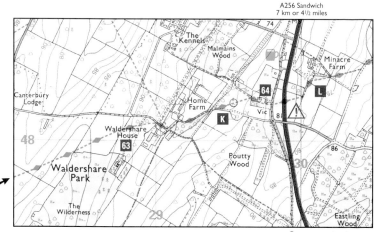

Contours are given in metres
The vertical interval is 5m

turn right **M**, along North Downs Close, keeping left through the fields.

Where the road comes to an end, a field-edge footpath continues straight onwards, keeping a hedge to your left. In the corner of the field, go over an iron ladder stile and into another field, keeping on the same line. Cross over the stile, and on to the Roman road. Turn right and pass a stile on the left. At the crossroads continue straight across, signposted to Whitfield and Dover. Where the metalled lane bears round to the right, you fork left on to the old Roman road between two forks into fields. Despite being an old Roman road, it is now just a narrow, sunken bridleway. Follow the line of the Roman road, although the path alignment is not arrow-straight.

Cross the road diagonally and continue along the track, still on the White Cliffs Country Trail. You soon arrive at the hamlet of Pineham. Where you meet the road, continue

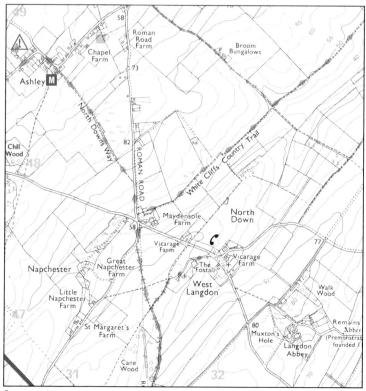

Contours are given in metres
The vertical interval is 5m

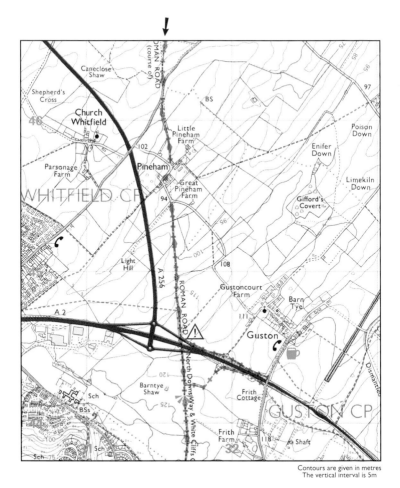

Contours are given in metres
The vertical interval is 5m

straight ahead, bearing a little to the right; do not take the
turning right, back on yourself, or left into the 'No Through
Road'. The road then bears a little to the left in front of a
barn and, just past the gate to Dane Cottages, where it
turns sharply to the left, you fork right on to the track. Go
through a gate, and up a drove road, which then becomes
a meadow-edge path with more gates. You go over the next
gate and stile and on to a drove road again, then the A2
comes into view.

When you arrive at the A2, turn right across the stiles
and follow the road edge to a flight of steps. Cross the A2
and two slip roads, turning left at the sign to take you to
a stile which once allowed you to walk straight over the
road when traffic was calmer. Alternative routes are being

looked at here. So follow the waymarking carefully. It is likely that the route will be diverted to the village of Guston, crossing the A2 on the smaller road bridge and removing the temptation for walkers to make a dash for it across the traffic. Suddenly, you can see the sea and then the Way starts to descend in a tunnel-like path beneath bushes. The track becomes a metalled lane, and you continue down the hill to Dover, crossing a loop of the railway line. Continue along the lane until you reach Old Charlton Road. Cross the road, go through a metalled railing alleyway and through the cemetery out on to Connaught Road. Turn left and the almost immediately right into Park Avenue. Continue along Park Avenue until you reach Maison Dieu Road at a five-pronged junction. (*Concluded on p. 158*).

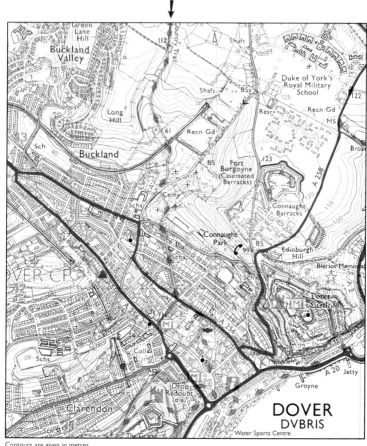

Contours are given in metres
The vertical interval is 5m

Turn left onto Maison Dieu Road and follow the road, passing a church on your left. Turn right into Pencester Road, past a bus garage and at the bus stop, turn left into the park. Cut across the park into Church Street. Continue along Church Street, with the church on your right and into King Street until you reach the Market Square. You have now completed the whole of the North Downs Way National Trail, an it is always a satisfying end to a long-distance route to finish at the coast.

Dover and the Romans

A mere 21 miles (34 km) of sea separates Dover from continental Europe, so it comes as no surprise that Julius Caesar chose beaches along this part of the Kent coast to land his expeditionary forces in 55 and 54 BC, nor that the town (*Dubris* to the Romans) continues to this day to be an important port for freight and passengers crossing the English Channel. Apart from London, Boulogne and Dover were the most important ports for this end of the Roman empire and, as a consequence, one of their network of roads through Britain –Watling Street –ran straight from Dover, through Canterbury to London, and then on into Shropshire. To guide the ships between Dover and Boulogne (a journey of eight hours' hard rowing), lighthouses, or pharos, were built; the one at Dover still stands beside St Mary-in-the-Castle Church in the grounds of Dover Castle and is claimed to be England's oldest building.

When, about 200 years after the birth of Christ, Rome felt the need to protect, in particular, the mineral wealth of Britain, a series of naval forts, known as the Forts of the Saxon Shore, were built, including one at Dover. Nearby stood what was effectively a luxurious hotel for the use of travelling officials of the Empire. In AD 270, when the Roman army took control of the fortress and extended it, part of the house was demolished and the rest of it buried beneath the new fortifications. It was this rapid burial of three rooms that kept them in a remarkable state of preservation for almost two millennia, until they were discovered in 1970 at the beginning of a programme of excavations carried out by the Kent Archaeological Rescue Unit. The Roman Painted House, as it is now known, was opened to the public in 1977 and, with its remarkably extensive areas of painted plaster, underfloor central heating system, and displays of many other contemporary finds, 'Britain's Buried Pompeii', as it is referred to in descriptive leaflets, is Dover's most popular tourist attraction.

Today's orchards, with their serried ranks of small, easy-to-manage trees, are a far cry from Kent's traditional 'garden yards'.

The orchards of Kent

The word 'orchard' probably derives from a combination of Latin and Old English words meaning roughly 'garden yard'. The North Downs Way will take you past and through a number of orchards as it makes its way through Kent, the 'Garden of England'. The traditional Kentish orchard with its mixture of large, standard, apple and pear trees, perhaps infilled with plums and other soft fruit, and even hedged by wind-breaking damson trees, is fast disappearing, although the Museum of Kent Life at Cobtree Manor Park near Maidstone is seeking to preserve it.

In this southern-eastern corner of England, Kent has been blessed with rich, deep soil, a mild, equable climate, and proximity to continental Europe as well as to the markets of London. It is not surprising, therefore, that the county should be one of the few where pears can be grown successfully and the only one that has commercial nut-growing, as well as the hardier and commoner fruits.

Because of their good keeping qualities, apples have long been used as a source of food, and both apples and pears are used to make alcoholic drinks. Apples have been cultivated for at least 3,000 years and, since Roman times, there have been orchards in Kent. Following the departure of the Romans, the monasteries continued the practice, but it was during the reign of Henry Tudor in the 16th century that fruit growing was carried out on a more commercial and organised basis. Although we might think of the 'traditional' Kentish orchards as having a long history, they are, in fact, remnants of a system that was begun as recently as the 19th century when amateur, as well as professional, growers were developing such typically English apples as the Cox's Orange Pippin or Laxton's Superb.

PART THREE

USEFUL
INFORMATION

Transport

Buses and Trains

Bus and train timetables are updated several times a year. Both Surrey and Kent County Councils produce excellent free guides and timetables to services which are available from the contacts below.

SURREY: Public Transport Group, Highways and Transportation Department, Surrey County Council, County Hall, Kingston-upon-Thames, Surrey KT1 2DN. Travel-line 01737 223000.

KENT: Highways and Transportation Department, Kent County Council, Springfield, Maidstone, Kent ME14 2LR. Tel: Freephone 0800 696996.

For further rail enquiries there is a national enquiry line Tel: 0345 484950. The following companies serve stations along the North Downs Way.

Network South Central Tel: 0345 484950. Serving: Farnham, Wanborough, Dorking, Boxhill and Westhumble, Merstham, Caterham, Oxted & Woldingham.

Thames Trains Tel: 0345 484950. Serving: Guildford, Shalford, Chilworth, Gomshall, Dorking West, Dorking, Deepdene, Betchworth, Reigate, Redhill.

Connex South Eastern Trains Tel: 0345 484950. Serving: Dunton Green, Otford, Kensington, Cuxton, Hollingbourne, Harrietsham, Lenham, Charing Wye, Chilham, Chartham, Canterbury West, Canterbury East, Bekesbourne, Sheperdswell, Dover Priory, Folkestone West, Folkestone Central.

Ferry Operators

Holyman Sally Ferries, Argyll Centre, York Street, Ramsgate CT11 9Ds. Tel: 0990 595522.

Hoverspeed, Marine Parade, Dover CT17 9TJ. Tel: 01394 249241.

P & O European Ferries, Channel View Road, Dover CT17 9TJ. Tel: 0990 980980.

Sea France: Eastern Docks, Dover, Kent CT16 1JA. Tel: 0990 711711.

Stena Line, Charter House, Park Street, Ashford TN24 8EX. Tel: 0990 707070.

Accommodation and Facilities

A practical handbook with information on over 800 facilities including pubs, shops, restaurants, attractions and accommodation is produced by North Downs Way Manager to complement this guide book. Copies are available from local bookshops in the area or by mail order on 01622 696037.

Two other useful publications are Stilwell's *National Trail Companion*, which contains an accommodation list for the North Downs Way and other long-distance walks and the *Ramblers Yearbook and Accommodation Guide* which includes bed and breakfast listings for the Way along with other useful information for walkers. Both are published annually and can be found in most bookshops, or the Ramblers' guide can be obtained direct from the Ramblers' Association, Tel: 0171 582 6878.

Tourist Information Centres

There are Tourist Information Centres at the following places close to the North Downs Way. These are useful for advice about local services and can usually book accommodation in advance.

Farnham, Vernon House, 25 West Street, Farnham, Surrey GU9 7BR. Tel: 01252 715109.

Guildford, The Undercroft, 14 Tunsgate, Guildford, Surrey GU1 3QT. Tel: 01483 444333.

Clackett Lane, Motorway Services Area, Clackett Lane, M25 Junction 5/6, Westerham, Kent TN16 2ER. Tel: 01959 565063/ 565615.

Sevenoaks, Buckhurst Lane, Sevenoaks, Kent TN13 1LQ. Tel: 01732 450305.

Rochester, Eastgate Cottage, High Street, Rochester, Kent ME1 1EW. Tel: 01634 843666.

Maidstone, The Gatehouse, Old Palace Gardens, Mill Street, Maidstone, Kent ME15 6YE. Tel: 01622 673581/602169.

Ashford, 18 The Churchyard, Ashford, Kent TN23 1QG. Tel: 01233 629165.

Folkestone, Harbour Street, Folkestone, Kent CT20 1QN. Tel: 01303 258 594.

Canterbury, 34 St Margaret's Street, Canterbury, Kent CT1 2TG. Tel: 01227 766567.

Dover, Burlington House, Townwall Street, Dover, Kent CT16 1JR. Tel: 01304 205108.

Useful addresses

North Downs Way Manager (Kent & Surrey), c/o Kent County Council, Planning Department, Springfield, Maidstone, Kent ME14 2LX. Tel: 01622 696185. Mail order (Tel: 01622 696037). Manages the development and promotion of the path.

Public Rights of Way Manager, Kent County Council, Highways Department, Standling Block, Springfield, Maidstone, Kent ME14 2LD. Tel: 01622 696921. Manages the practical maintenance of the path in Kent.

Public Rights of Way Manager, Surrey County Council, Environment, County Hall, Kingston-upon-Thames, Surrey KT1 2DM Tel: 0181 541 8800. Manages the practical maintenance of the path in Surrey.

Weather check, Kent and Surrey area. Tel: 0891 112250.

British Horse Society, Regional Development Officer, 4 Hill View Crescent, Orpington, Kent BR6 0SL. Tel: 01689 872747. Promotes the upkeep of bridleways and encourages safety and training of horses and riders.

British Trust for Conservation Volunteers, South Area Office, Southwater Country Park, Cripplegate Lane, Southwater, West Sussex RH13 7UN. Tel: 01403 730 572. Organises practical conservation projects.

Byways & Bridleways Trust, St Mary's Business Centre, Oystershell Lane, Newcastle-upon-Tyne NE4 5QS. Tel: 0191 2330770. Protects and develops byways, bridleways & public rights of way in general.

Countryside Commission, Headquarters, John Dower House, Crescent Place, Cheltenham, Glos, GL50 3RA. Tel: 01242 521381. The official government body on countryside matters.

Countryside Commission, South East Region, 71 Kingsway, London, WC2B 6ST. Tel: 0171 831 3510.

Countryside Commission, Postal Sales, PO Box 124, Wargrave, Northampton NN6 9TL. Tel: 01604 781848.

Cyclists Touring Club, 69 Meadrow, Godalming, Surrey, GU7 3HS. Tel: 01483 417217. Represents cyclists in matters affecting use of roads and access to the countryside.

English Heritage, Fortress House, 23 Savile Road, London W1X 1AB. Tel: 0171 973 3000. The official government body on England's historic built heritage.

English Nature, South East Region, Cold Harbour Farm, Wye, Ashford, Kent TN25 5OB. Tel: 01233 812525. The official government body on nature conservation in England.

England Tourist Board, Thames Tower, Blacks Road, Hammersmith, London W6 9EL. Tel: 0181 8469000.

South East England Tourist Board, The Old Brew House, Warwick Park, Tunbridge Wells, Kent TN2 5TU. Tel: 01892 540766.

Federation Francaise de la Randonnée Pedestre, 358, rue des Glycines, 62110 Henin-Beaumont, France. Tel: 00 333 21205912.

Kent Wildlife Trust, Tyland Barn, Sandling, Maidstone, Kent ME14 3BD. Tel: 01622 662012. County wildlife protection group.

Long Distance Walkers' Association, c/o Les Maple, 21 Upcroft, Windsor, Berkshire SL43 3NH. Tel: 01753 866685. Furthers the interests of long-distance walkers.

Motorised Land Access and Recreational Association, PO Box 9, Cannock, Staffs. WS11 2FE. Tel: 01543 467218. Promote vehicles access on rights of way.

The town of Guildford, with its cathedral and university, is situated on a gap cut through the North Downs by the River Wey.

National Trust (Kent Regional Information), c/o Scotney Castle, Lamberhurst, Tunbridge Wells, Kent, TN3 8JN. Protects through ownership, countryside, coastland and many historic buildings in England.

National Trust (Surrey Regional Information), c/o Polesden Lacey, Dorking, Surrey, RH5 6BD.

National Trust (Shop & Information Centre), Box Hill Road, Box Hill, Tadworth, Surrey KT20 7LB. Tel: 01306 888793.

Ordnance Survey, Romsey Road, Southampton, Hants SO16 4GU. Tel: 0345 330011. National Mapping Agency of Great Britain.

Ramblers Association, 1–5 Wandsworth Road, London, SW8 2XX. Tel: 0171 5826878. Promotes walking, protects right of way, and defends the beauty of the countryside.

Surrey Wildlife Trust, School Lane, Pirbright, Woking, Surrey, GU24 0JN. Tel: 01483 488055. County wildlife protection group.

Youth Hostels Association, Trevelyan House, 8 St Stephens Hill, St Albans, Herts, AL1 2DY. Tel: 01727 855215. Low-cost hostel accommodation for young people.

Other walks

There are many other excellent walks in the South-eastern region. Three other National Trails are nearby – The South Downs Way, a 99-mile (159 km) path between Winchester and Eastbourne, The Ridgeway, a 85-mile (137 km) path from Overton Hill near Avebury to Ivinghoe Beacon, east of Tring; and the Thames Path, a 180-mile (288 km) path from the rivers source in Gloucestershire to the Thames Barrier in London. There are official guides to all three, produced by Aurum Press in the same series as this one.

For more information contact:

The South Downs Way Manager, Sussex Down Conservation Board, Chanctonbury House, Stanmer Park, Lewes Road, Brighton BN1 9SE. Tel: 01273 625242.

The Ridgeway/Thames Path Manager, the National Trails Office, Countryside Service, Department of Leisure and Arts, Holton, Oxford OX33 1QQ. Tel: 01865 810224.

Kent County Council produce a publications catalogue with guides to over 100 promoted routes in the county which is available free from: Judith Roberts, c/o Planning Department, Springfield, Maidstone, Kent ME14 2LX. Tel: 01622 696037.

There are several circular walks which have been developed along the North Downs Way linking to local pubs and other recreation routes in Kent. Information on these is also available from Kent County Council.

Surrey County Council produce a list of countryside publications which include walk-packs, event programmes and circular paths. The list is available free from: Linda Calver, c/o Environment Department, County Hall, Kingston-upon-Thames, Surrey KT1 2DN. Tel: 0181 541 9463.

The North Downs Way is part of the European footpath network linking Britain to mainland Europe, for more details on walks in France contact the French rambling association equivalent: Federation Francaise de la Randonnée Pedestre, 64 rue de Gergorie F-75014 Paris. Tel: 0033 45453102.

Bibliography

Adair, John, *The Pilgrims Way: shrines and saints in Britain and Ireland* (Thames and Hudson, 1978).

Allen, David J. and Imrie, Patrick R., *Discovering the North Downs Way* (Shire Publications, 1980).

Belloc, Hilaire, *The Old Road* (Constable, 1904).

Castle, Alan, *Long Distance Paths South East England* (A & C Black, 1990).

Charles, Alan, *Exploring the Pilgrims Way* (Countryside Books, 1992).

Cobbet, William, *Rural Rides* (Penguin, 1967).

Hall, D. J., *English Medieval Pilgrimages* (Routledge, 1966).

Hawell, John, *Walk the North Downs* (Bartholomew Map & Guide, 1987).

Westacott, H. D., *The North Downs Way* (Penguin, 1983).

Wright, C. J. A., *Guide to the Pilgrims' Way and North Downs Way* (Constable, 1971).

Ordnance Survey Maps covering the North Downs Way

Landranger Maps (scale: 1:50,000): 177, 178, 179, 186, 187, 188, 189.

Explorer Maps (scale 1:25,000): 137 (Ashford, Headcorn, Chilham and Wye), 138 (Dover, Folkestone and Hythe), 145 (Guildford and Farnham, Godalming and Farnborough), 146 (Dorking, Box Hill and Reigate), 147 (Sevenoaks and Tonbridge, Royal Tunbridge Wells), 148 (Maidstone and the Medway Towns), 149 (Sittingbourne and Faversham, Isle of Sheppey), 150 (Canterbury and the Isle of Thanet), 163 (Gravesend and Rochester, Hoo Peninsula).

Motoring Maps (scale 1:250,000: Reach the North Downs Way by using Travelmaster 9 'South East England'.